D0294912

THE DAY OF RECKONING

The Day of Reckoning, 1883. Samuel Edmund Waller (1850–1903)
If the lady and gentleman had been wearing the clothes of their own period, how much more acceptable this picture would be today! The house in the background is based on Kirby Hall, near Corby, Northamptonshire, which now stands among opencast mines, a magnificent ruin cared for by the Ministry of Works.

THE
DAY
OF
RECKONING

✳✳✳✳✳✳✳✳✳✳✳

by

MARY CLIVE

THE REPRINT SOCIETY LONDON

FIRST PUBLISHED 1964
THIS EDITION PUBLISHED BY THE REPRINT SOCIETY LTD, 1965
BY ARRANGEMENT WITH MACMILLAN & CO LTD
Copyright © Mary Clive 1964

By the same author
Christmas with the Savages

PRINTED IN GREAT BRITAIN
BY JOHN SWAIN AND SON LIMITED, BARNET

Contents

✳✳✳✳✳✳✳✳✳✳✳✳✳✳✳✳✳✳✳✳✳✳✳✳✳✳✳✳✳✳✳✳✳✳✳✳✳

CONTENTS

Illustrations

�֎�֎✖✖

CHAPTER FIVE

CHAPTER SIX

CHAPTER SEVEN

CHAPTER EIGHT

CHAPTER NINE

CHAPTER TEN

FINALE

Bibliography

✳✳

The *Dictionary of National Biography*; *The Times* obituary column; *Who's Who*; *Who Was Who*; *Who's Who in Art*; *The Royal Academy of Arts, 1769–1904* (Algernon Graves); Catalogue of the Chantrey Exhibition at Burlington House, 1949; *Painters of the Victorian Scene* (Graham Reynolds, Batsford, 1953).

Various memoirs and biographies of artists, especially the following: *The Tale of Beatrix Potter* (Margaret Lane, F. Warne, 1946); *An Autobiography* (Lady Butler, Constable, 1922); *Kate Greenaway* (M. H. Spielman and G. S. Layard, A. and C. Black, 1905); *Two Nobles Lives:* Louisa Marchioness of Waterford and her Sister (Augustus Hare, George Allen, 1893); *Florence Upton, Painter* (Edith Lyttleton, Longmans, Green, 1926); *The Strange World of Alfred Rethel* (*The Times*, 1 December, 1959).

So Kind to Youth by Evelyn Ball (Michael Joseph, 1939) includes an amusing if highly-coloured account of what it felt like to be one of Marcus Stone's models.

During the eighties and nineties the *Art Annual* (Virtue) issued illustrated monographs on popular living artists, and in the early numbers of *The Strand Magazine* there are interviews with prominent Academicians. The illustrated catalogues of the Royal Academy Summer Exhibitions provide a panorama of the ordinary taste of any particular year and back numbers of *The Studio* show what was admired by those interested in the arts. Arthur Mee's *Children's Encyclopaedia* is a mine of narrative pictures and has a good index, and Victorian encyclopaedias sometimes give biographies of painters whose reputations have now slumped. Useful articles can also be discovered in the files of *Country Life*.

Acknowledgements

❋❋❋

I am most grateful to the galleries, firms, periodicals and individuals who have allowed me to reproduce copyright material, and to all the people who have lent pictures, sent information or helped in other ways. In addition to those whose names are in the list of illustrations I must mention the Hon. Edward Biddulph, Mr. Wilfred Blunt, the Dean of Brecon, Brigadier Clive, Mrs. J. B. Cole, Lady Craik, the Earl of Cromer, Mr. F. E. Cronshaw, the Dowager Lady Dunsany, Messrs Fores of Bond Street, Miss Cecily Hacon, Mrs. Oriana Haynes, Messrs Heywood Hill, the Rev. Mother of the Priory of Our Lady, Burford, Mrs. Philip de László, Miss Irene Lee Warner, Mr. J. McNeile, Miss Mary NcNeile, Miss F. Pomeroy, and Miss Yootha Rose.

Mrs. William Phipps collected most of the illustrations. Messrs A. C. Cooper took about half the photographs and were undaunted by some very unpromising material. Mr. Donovan Wilson, A.I.B.P., of Hereford, helped me out on four occasions. Miss Peggy Sutton typed the manuscript. Miss C.-A. Parker of the Royal Academy Library was of the utmost assistance, and the London Library was of course invaluable.

The quotations from Lady Butler's memoirs are by permission of Messrs Constable and Co Ltd; the passage from *The Dolly Dialogues*, by Anthony Hope, by permission of the Trustees of the Hope Hawkins Estate and Messrs Methuen and Co Ltd; the passage from *Dodo*, by E. F. Benson, by permission of the author's Executor and Messrs Methuen and Co Ltd; and the lines from 'The Shooting of Dan McGrew', from *Songs of a Sourdough*, by Robert Service, by permission of Messrs Ernest Benn Ltd.

In a few cases I have not been able to trace the owners of copyrights and to them I apologize.

Artists

Passenger Pigeons

AT the beginning of the last century the American passenger pigeon was the most abundant bird in the world. Flocks of them, two billion strong, flew overhead darkening the sun. . . . In 1914 the last one died in a Cincinnati zoo and the race became extinct. Many everyday objects suffer the same fate as the passenger pigeon. Excessively common at one moment, a little later they are nowhere to be found.

In this book I have attempted to resuscitate some of the commonplaces of my childhood, things which we took for granted as a permanent part of civilized life and which have now been pushed into the shadows. I admit that my home was not an average home, but then, who does have an average home? Other children grew up in other surroundings. This was the world of one female child some fifty years ago.

CHAPTER ONE

White Muslin and Blue Ribbons

WE are back at the beginning of the long reign of George V, when the present felt bright and light and safe and prosaic, and history was definitely over, and nothing exciting would ever happen again. I could imagine no future of any sort particularly as I was hourly expecting the last trump with the possibility of finding myself in a fiery hell. (A learned judge had already 'dismissed hell with costs', but it still hung round the Church of England like a bad smell which, if taken no notice of, might fade away of its own accord.) The past, rainbow-hued and heroic, peopled by beautiful princesses and sympathetic knights, *that* was the interesting time. Horatius, Boadicea, King Alfred and Margaret-and-the-Robbers were my intimate friends, far more amenable as well as more colourful than my contemporaries.

Between history and myself stretched the dark tunnel in which the grown-ups had lived when they were young. According to their own accounts they had been very uncomfortable in it. Conditions, they said, were spartan, rules strict, parents stern; and they repeatedly told us that we were very lucky indeed to be us and not them, a statement which for once we did not dispute.

This dark tunnel must have been full of a sort of brown smoke because the things which came out of it, like photographs, books, clothes and even some of the people themselves, were tinged with brown round the edges and had a peculiar, fusty smell. Once the Universe had got inside the tunnel, it groped its way forward enveloped in brown-ness until suddenly (presumably at sunrise on 1 January, 1900) it blundered out into the daylight, and nowadays began. (I am not trying to be whimsical. This was how the past looked to me in 1913 and how, to a large extent, it looks to me still.)

As I grew older I often ruminated over the word 'nowadays' and thought what an odd chance it was that instead of being born a savage painted with woad or an Ancient Greek, I was saved up until the year 1907 A.D. and plumped right into the middle of nowadays. Human beings had had to make a long plod uphill and at least, here we were at the—no, not exactly the top, but at the *right* level. Normal, in fact. I was not unique in this attitude and many older and wiser persons took it for granted that, though far from perfect, we had got the world fixed more or less as God had originally intended it to be, and that every effort must be made to keep it so. Did not Warren Harding, in 1921, become President of the United States with the war-cry, 'Back to Normalcy!' What is more, one could find many elderly people today who feel that since 1914 the world has never

1906

Some of my relations the year before I was born. One saw many photographs like this but, by the time I can remember, ladies showed their good taste by dressing more drably.

Bookplate, 1906

Edwardiana

managed to be 'normal' again and they sigh for divinely inspired Edwardian prices.

But what about that mysterious bit of nowadays that had taken place *after* the world had come out of the dark tunnel but *before* I was born? We used to spend the summer in a big rambling house in Ireland, the furniture of which had obviously been there a very long time—old-fashioned, the nurses not unfairly called it—and yet I could see that it was sprinkled with things which were neither ancient nor modern, and I got an idea that there had been for a short time a gloriously gay interval when my mother and aunts wore billowy white dresses which trailed on the grass, and everyday objects were made in materials and colours that were pretty rather than practical. (Hooray!) One could only suppose that the staid elders, wild with delight at getting out of the shades, had indulged in a burst of reckless giddiness before settling down to plain, dull normalcy.

My mother was married just at the turn of the century and some of her belongings were absolutely out of character and not the sort of thing that came into the house any more. She had, for instance, a white walking-stick with a pink marble knob, and little boxes that looked so luscious that I longed to eat them. The grape-scissors were encrusted with vine leaves and there were books of poetry in rich fanciful bindings. She particularly disapproved of nudity and yet nymphs and cupids had crept in; there were cupids on her bookplate and the silver fern-pot in the middle of the dining-room table was embossed with bacchantes. Was it she who chose those chintzes and wallpapers (already slightly faded) festooned with pink roses and fluttering blue ribbons? It could not have been Granny— one had only to look at her to see that—so it must have been my mother.

She was not at all a fluffy type and yet her bedroom was white and frilly. The dressing-table was draped in muslin flounces and on the chaise-longue were frilled muslin cushions embroidered with baskets of flowers, monograms and coronets. The sweetpeas and gypsophila were in a glass vase shaped like an inverted mob-cap and decorated with gold sprays (it was put into the corridor at night, of course, otherwise instant death would result). There was a white fur hearthrug and the walls were papered with white watered-silk paper topped by an exquisite frieze of mauve wistaria. I thought it unutterably lovely and I was aware that it was, as shops say, a discontinued line.

The pictures, too, were just a trifle passé. We did not think much of Briton Riviere's lions—not his well-known Daniel but just lions sitting about by themselves doing nothing. My eldest sister tried to make them more interesting by the suggestion that a smudge on the horizon was a traveller who would eventually get eaten, but it did not catch on. Then there was a caricature of my father in polo clothes; and a relic of his Oxford days, a picture which we all liked, called *Death as a Friend*. I still think this shows a sensible and cheering attitude towards an important subject. Down with the ostriches who do not allow death to be referred to under any circumstances and down with the croaking ravens who only relish symbolism when the meaning is disagreeable! We also approved of a stipple engraving after Reynolds, *Venus Chiding Cupid for Learning to Cast Accounts*. The Bartolozzi style usually made me feel impatient, almost ill, but this was an exception because of the intriguing dash of worldly cynicism.

The largest picture hung over the bed (iron with brass knobs) and was called *The Day*

The Queen Victoria Memorial outside Buckingham Palace. Sculpted by Sir Thomas Brock, R.A. (1847–1922)

Rightly or wrongly, Victoria's name became a synonym for prudishness, yet when she died 'they' commissioned a monument swarming with nudes. It was unveiled in 1911 by which time George V was on the throne, and my mother, who was among the vast crowds present, used to declare that when the sheet dropped there was a gasp of horror. However, *The Times* made no mention of this, so it may have been her imagination.

Sympathy. Briton Riviere, R.A. (1840–1920) (Tate Gallery) Another version of this once-popular picture is in the Royal Holloway College Gallery. 'The little girl was painted from my daughter, Miss Millicent A. Riviere. The dog, with some slight alterations (as my animals are never portraits) was done from a bull-terrier belonging to a man who has supplied me with dogs for some considerable time.'

Briton Riviere succeeded Landseer as top animal painter, his speciality being lions. He illustrated various Bible stories and his two Daniel pictures were much reproduced. So, too, was his *Gadarene Swine. Lazarus and canine friends,* though equally lifelike, were less often seen.

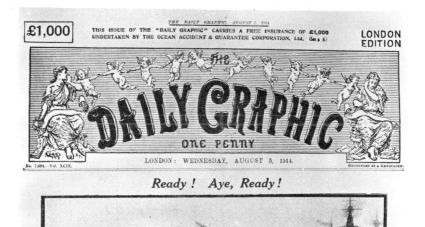

THE DAILY GRAPHIC, AUGUST 5, 1914

£1,000

THIS ISSUE OF THE "DAILY GRAPHIC" CARRIES A FREE INSURANCE OF £1,000 UNDERTAKEN BY THE OCEAN ACCIDENT & GUARANTEE CORPORATION, Ltd. (See p. 6)

LONDON EDITION

THE DAILY GRAPHIC

ONE PENNY

LONDON: WEDNESDAY, AUGUST 5, 1914.

No. 7,684.—Vol. XCIX.

REGISTERED AS A NEWSPAPER.

Ready! Aye, Ready!

of Reckoning.

'What does it mean?' we asked.

'Can't you guess?' said my mother.

We looked again. People standing about round a front door. Horses, dogs, grooms. A familiar sort of scene but nothing much happening.

'What about the auctioneer?' said my mother.

We then perceived the auctioneer and wondered how he came to be allowed so close to the house. My mother wondered how she came to have such stupid children.

To her the whole story was as clear as crystal. The young man had ruined himself gambling, racing, playing billiards, backing bills and was now being sold up. It was a very usual predicament. She had met the young man in countless novels and knew a poem by Samuel Johnson about him. 'Loosened from the minor's tether, Free to mortgage or to sell, Wild as wind and light as feather, Bid the sons of thrift farewell.' She had even learnt, perhaps from the same poem, something to the disadvantage of the prissy-looking woman behind him, at least she pointedly referred to her as 'the sister'.

This piece of life-in-the-raw, so vivid and exciting to my mother, left us stone cold. That sort of rake was out-of-date. Ruined? To us the word meant Monte Carlo. The Count staggered out of the garish rooms to borrow a revolver or to join the bodies hanging from the trees in the public gardens. One could not be ruined in the calm light of an English morning with one's sister beside one. However, rather than go into all that, we attacked from the flank; we said the house was absurd, those windows were impossible. My mother hotly defended the windows and here she was on firmer ground than she knew because as a matter of fact the house was drawn from a real stately home in the Shires.

The two generations bickered away, unable to appreciate the other's point of view. In

7

Death as a Friend. (Woodcut.) Alfred Rethel
(1816–1859)

From a print in the Victoria & Albert Museum
This forgotten German artist was formerly so
famous that he was allotted a whole column in
the *Encyclopaedia Britannica*. When young he
made his name with large historical frescoes.
Later, becoming unhinged, he turned to the
macabre. *Death the Avenger* is said to have
driven insane a man with a guilty secret who
won it in a lottery. *Death as a Friend*, on the
other hand, is calm and reassuring.

'*And When Did You Last See Your Father?*' 1878. W. F. Yeames, R.A. (1836–1918)
(Walker Art Gallery, Liverpool)

At Madame Tussaud's the tableau of this enthralling scene still holds its own in spite of newer attractions.
Perhaps its popularity is due to the fact that one is quite sure that the brave little boy is a match for all
the wicked Roundheads.

the eighties and nineties the appeal of this picture had been so immediate and general that no country house was complete without it; and now, a decade or two later, it failed even to tell its story. We dismissed it as boring.

(' You are not to say "boring",' said my mother.)

★   ★   ★

Where have they hidden themselves, those enormous framed and glazed reproductions of *The Day of Reckoning*? And if one wanted to have another look at that memorable scene, where would one turn?

Formerly one would have gone straight to Mansells in Oxford Street. It was on a corner, about opposite Selfridge's, and it stocked sepia reproductions of famous pictures, from *Mona Lisa* to '*And When Did You Last See Your Father?*' Gone, too, or modernized beyond recognition, are the other picture shops which used to display such a rivetting jumble in their windows—the head of Christ with closed eyes which presently began looking at you,* next to *Three Blind Mice* lying dead drunk beside an overturned wineglass. Did they all vanish in a night? Or did they drop off the hooks one by one? It is a mystery like the disappearance of the smell of musk; but gone they are now and there are no sepia landscapes of rustic bridges and thatched cottages, except in junk shops.

I went around asking my friends whether they remembered *The Day of Reckoning* and several claimed to do so though some were obviously thinking of *The Last Day in the Old Home* and one man said, 'Ah, yes, *The Rake's Progress* . . .'. My sister had seen it no longer ago than last summer in the dining-room of a small hotel near the Roman Wall, and I heard of another copy in an attic in Wiltshire, only it was so large that there could be no question of getting it into a car to bring it to me. The group on the right, I was told, if looked at from a discreet distance, turns into a Highlander.

The most helpful person was my mother's old friend, Mrs. B., who is in the eighty-plus age group. 'By Samuel Edmund Waller,' she said without a moment's hesitation.

It was easy then to go to the London Library and look up Waller in the *Dictionary of National Biography*, and having found the date of his death, hunt out his obituary notice in *The Times*. He was also in Graves' *Royal Academy*, which lists the pictures exhibited by every artist from its commencement to 1904. This catalogue, though limited in its appeal, is invaluable for anyone interested in obscure British painters and at auctions it fetches round about £140.

Gradually I collected a few facts. Samuel Edmund Waller was born in 1850. He was the son of the architect in charge of Gloucester Cathedral and had some training in his father's office. Like many other Victorians he developed early, exhibiting in the Royal Academy at the age of twenty-one. He had always had a passion for drawing horses and he subsequently

*By Gabriell Max. *b.* Prague 1840, *d.* Munich 1915.

became famous for his pictures of country-house life in the olden time, scenes in which animals could be combined with architecture. Waller's grandparents lived at Burford in the Cotswolds, and the manor houses of the surrounding district can be detected in many of his backgrounds. For instance, the picture called *The Empty Saddle*, followed by eight lines of poetry beginning 'But, oh, the bitter tears we wept . . .', includes the notable façade of Burford Priory, while the house in *The Day of Reckoning* is Kirby Hall, Northamptonshire. The derelict mansion in *Home? There was no sign of home from parapet to basement. Hood*, which went to the National Gallery of New South Wales and which depicts a horseman who, returning from perhaps the Grand Tour, finds deer grazing round his front door, is also obviously drawn from another Cotswold manor. This mixture of houses and horses was irresistible and Waller's pictures became 'well-known by reproductions and engravings throughout the English-speaking world', and two were included in the collection which Sir Henry Tate threw in when he presented the Tate Gallery to the Nation.

And that was about all I could discover, except that his niece remembers him as being a vivid creature and an unparalleled companion, and that his wife also painted, and that after a long illness he died in 1903.

So then I nerved myself to sidle into the library of the Royal Academy feeling rather sheepish to be making enquiries about an artist who was so very *démodé*, but a kind and charming girl showed me a catalogue-scrapbook of the 1883 Exhibition, and at last I was able to feast my eyes on Waller's smash hit. How nice to see them all again—the young man and his sister, the horses and dogs and the grooms, even, with a little imagination, the Highlander. Nevertheless, it was hard to perceive what precise quality this particular scene possessed to enable it to outsoar all the similar pictures that were being painted at the same time;—could it merely have been the serve-him-right slant of the title which enabled worthy citizens who never gambled and backed bills to enjoy the disaster without having to feel sorry for the victim?

Also in the scrapbook were a few modest remarks by Waller himself. He made the point that his sort of picture was very expensive to produce. For example, in *One and Twenty* there were seven horses and fourteen people, and the horse bill was £25 and the human models cost more than £35. On top of that there was £15 for the costumes and £30 for the frame, and there were payments to an architectural draughtsman for a scale model of the building—he could have done it himself but it would have been a waste of his time. And then he had had to journey into Wales to make a sketch of the park. . . .

My mother would have been pleased to hear that he had gone to so much trouble. She often used to say, looking at a modern picture with contempt, '*That* can't have taken him long'.

10

CHAPTER TWO

Calming Down

❀❀❀

I WAS born in London, in a tall house in Bryanston Square which my parents had recently acquired. It was one of those houses which seem to be all stairs and no rooms. White paint was much in evidence, glossy off-white or broken-white, not the dead flat white which was the background of our home in Ireland. I remember with particular affection the china door handles and finger-plates decorated with bright little bunches of flowers. Such things are back in fashion again after a long spell of neglect but I do not think the modern ones are as pretty as those we had in our nursery.

The front drawing-room had double doors into the back room, and three french windows leading onto a balcony that was too dirty to use and looking out onto the trees of the Square. It was like thousands of other London drawing-rooms, light and pleasant, not cosy. The décor was mid-Edwardian, that is to say Edwardian sobered up, calmed down, cooled off. Exuberance was *out* and though we still had garlands of roses, their petals were less pink and their leaves less green. Muslin and blue ribbons only were seen when the children came down after tea. The prevailing colours were mushroom and fawn and a certain amount of gold. The style could be called Louis, a restrained sort of Louis. It was just the room for callers.

I cannot quite place these callers. Presumably they were young marrieds, though I did not, and do not, connect them with the adjective 'young'. They rustled and chirruped in and they rustled and chirruped out again. They wore big hats and veils and feather boas, and they carried lorgnettes and parasols.

A few of the children we knew had kitten-type mothers, little women with lustrous hair coiled round their heads and simple clinging gowns, perhaps cerulean to match their eyes. They wore very white powder which made their skin look mauve and which came off on our faces when they kissed us; and they smelt of scent. The villainess of children's books was often a Fashionable Mother whom we believed in but never expected to meet. It did not cross our minds to equate them with the kittens who were very sweet to their children and called them 'Darling' in cooing voices. The other callers were so unglamorous one assumed they were virtuous. We had, indeed, a proper horror of the world of fashion and I can remember how shocked I was when my mother, who usually dressed in the same way as she had always dressed, appeared at lunch in one of the high collars I had seen in an advertisement. For a moment my faith in her respectability tottered.

Among the grown-ups there was also an occasional *enfant terrible*, women who threw

1923. Mrs Stanley Baldwin
and friend

1912. At the Horticultural Hall
Lady Westbury, the Hon. **Lady Rivers Wilson and**
Lady Lilford; all three were in their early fifties.

1959. Costermonger

Young socialites at a charity sale, November 1913
Duchess of Sutherland, Lady Rosemary Leveson-Gower, Miss de
Trafford, Miss Millington Drake, Lady Sybil Grey.

Paris Fashion, September 1913

In the first quarter of the century fashions changed more violently than they have done in the last twenty-five years, and women who had not the nerve to follow them soon got very much left behind. There were, however, plenty of shops which obligingly stocked expensive frumpswear, and between the wars callers continued to appear in clothes that were practically Edwardian.

Early 1900s   1926   1939

During the last forty years fashions have gone round in circles, so that the grandmother of today who dresses much as she did when she was a girl looks passably modern and not like a real granny.

'Dodo'
Mrs. Asquith (1864–1945) dressed as a snake-charmer at a fancy-dress ball at Devonshire House in 1897.

13

into the conversation saucy or daring remarks which made a splash and produced squeaks of 'Oh, *Maud!*' or '*Really* Blanche!' or even 'Edith! You *are!*' Behind their backs their friends, somewhat acidly, said things like 'Millicent *would*'. As they got older they grew, if anything, more *terrible*, and eventually they turned into the sort of old lady who looks very conventional but who makes a point of saying whatever comes into her head, sometimes with comic effect, sometimes giving great offence.

I suppose the saucy type had its greatest vogue in late Victorian times when quantities of self-confident American girls arrived in Europe and seemed wonderfully bright and amusing, sophisticated and emancipated, elegant and well-dressed, beside the snubbed and down-trodden English debutantes. I had three American great-aunts, all married for love and the two I knew personally were very vivacious talkers whose sayings were quoted round the family with varying degrees of admiration—but, indeed, one was always meeting lively American women married to quiet admiring Englishmen.

The most famous *enfant terrible* in fiction was E. F. Benson's Dodo (1893) who was supposed to be modelled on Margot Tennant, afterwards Lady Oxford and Asquith. Dodo was considered naughty but fascinating, and this is how she chattered to her good, kind, husband, Lord Chesterford, the morning after the old family friend had refused to elope with her. They are going out hunting and the time is soon after six a.m.

Dodo was not conscious of the least embarrassment and determined to do her duty.

'Morning, old boy,' she said, 'you look as sleepy as a d.p. or dead pig. Look at my hat. It's a new hat, Chesterford, and is the joy of my heart. Isn't it sweet? Have some tea and give me another kidney—two, I think. What happens to the sheep after they take its kidneys out? Do you suppose it dies? I wonder if they put india rubber kidneys in. Kidneys do come from sheep, don't they? Or is there a kidney tree? Kidneys look like a sort of mushroom, and I suppose the bacon is the leaves, Kidnonia Baconiensis. . . .'

(And she continued in this manner for nearly another page.)

Chesterford laughed. Dodo had not behaved like this for months. What did it all mean? But the events of the night before were too deeply branded on his memory to let him comfort himself very much. But anyhow it was charming to see Dodo like this again. And she shall never know.

You can imagine how tiresome imitators of Dodo might become, especially when they grew older and less good-looking.

An exact contemporary of Dodo was Dolly of Anthony Hope's *Dolly Dialogues*. She was a saucy little minx rather than a true *enfant terrible* and she was lighter than Dodo. On the other hand, she was almost impossible to imitate as she depended on a partner to do half the backchat, while Dodo was essentially a soliloquist, so though doubtless many girls aspired to be a Dolly, I cannot remember meeting one who was actually in the least like her.

★　　　　　★　　　　　★

But to go back to our drawing-room in Bryanston Square.

It was after tea and there was no one there but the children in their clean muslin frocks, building a Tower of Babel with the never-palling drawing-room bricks. My mother had finished reading the day's ration of *Captains Courageous* and someone started talking about the pictures. The one I liked was a water-colour of a rose pergola which had a gold mount and was the only really bright object in the room. My mother then pointed out two which she admired. They were tall and thin, a shape much favoured by late Victorian academic artists as well as by Sickert, and they fitted in nicely between the french windows and their colours toned in very well with the curtains.

We stared at them. One, she said, was called *Love and Death*. Well, we could all understand that. We were quite accustomed to stories in which silent veiled white strangers were confronted by another apparition who claimed that his or her name was Love. The only interesting point was which of them was going to get the best of it.

My mother did not seem to know and she invited us to guess the subject of the other picture. One man standing by himself and no clues at all.

'I see a venerable character,' began my sister, ever ready to accept a challenge, 'perhaps even the Venerable Bede.'

'Nonsense,' said my mother. 'It's quite a young man. Now what is he wearing?'

'Sort of a dressing-gown.'

'Oh, come! It's rather a fine robe with a fur collar. And what is he doing?'

'Looking for something on the ground.'

'No, no, he's going away sorrowing. He's the young man with great possessions—in the Bible—you must remember.'

Yes, I remembered, and I wondered how my mother could, how she *could*, bear to have him in her drawing-room. The passage in which he occurs had always seemed to me the most uncomfortable in the whole New Testament. To forgive your enemies, to be meek,

'How should you describe me, then?' she asked, leaning forward with a smile.

'I should describe you, Lady Mickleham,' I replied discreetly, 'as being a little lower than the angels.'

Dolly's smile was almost a laugh as she asked:

'How much lower, please, Mr. Carter?'

'Just the depth of your dimples,' said I, thoughtlessly. Dolly became immensely grave.

'I thought,' said she, 'that we never mentioned them now, Mr. Carter.'

'Did we ever?' I asked innocently.

'I seem to remember once; do you recollect being in very low spirits one evening at Monte?'

'I remember being in very low water more than one evening there.'

from *The Dolly Dialogues*, by Anthony Hope
(Sir Anthony Hawkins, 1863–1933, author of
The Prisoner of Zenda)

patient, merciful, was absolute child's play; but to give all your goods to the poor—no, not that, not that.

How could my mother and her callers bear to sit in front of such a picture, among the bibelots and the French furniture? Was it just another fairy tale, something that it would be silly to take seriously? Not a tenth of one's goods, not half, not even three-quarters, but *all!*

There was already at the back of my mind a dark suspicion. The grown-ups had made us learn the Ten Commandments and recite, 'Remember that thou keep holy the Sabbath Day. . . . In it thou shalt do no manner of work, thou, and thy son, and thy daughter, thy manservant and thy maidservant. . . .' We children were made to spend puritanical Sundays—no cards, no tennis, no sewing, no going in the car or travelling by train. The servants, it is true, worked slightly less than usual, and yet they cooked the meals and served them, made the beds, lit the fires and answered the bell. Did the grown-ups only obey the Bible so long as it suited them to do so; and when its fiats were inconvenient, did they just ignore them? It seems they did. And if it was legitimate to jettison a portion of the Fourth Commandment because it was tiresome, why not the whole of the other nine?

In some form or other thousands of my contemporaries were asking themselves similar questions and coming to the conclusion that the religion of the Victorians was a sham, mere convention, a matter of form only. They grew up to vote Labour, to preach free love and atheism, to be rebels and debunkers, above all to be cynics—not pretended cynics, but genuine ones. Utterly disillusioned in fact.

The grown-ups were pained and surprised. They simply could not see what the fuss was about. 'So unnecessary' was the expression they used.

$\star$ $\star$ $\star$

(*Maple & Co.*)

I was somewhat older—quite eleven in fact—before I was taken to the Tate Gallery and was free to wander in the enormous room at that time entirely devoted to the works of the artist Watts. My sister and I were in the first flush of a craze for art and we tore round shouting, from *Mammon* to *Life's Illusions*, welcoming *Love and Death* and *For He Had Great Possessions* as old friends, my conscience not giving me the smallest twinge. We were happy in the belief that Watts was a very great master and we took his messages on trust, assuming that they were meant for what my uncle would have called 'the other fellow'. How satisfactory it was to find an artist with whom one could feel perfectly safe, who managed to be powerful, uplifting, entertaining, and at the same time un-coarse, and eminently drawing-room-worthy !

For He Had Great Possessions. G. F. Watts.
(Tate Gallery)

17

CHAPTER THREE

Utter Normalcy

✳✳

IN 1911 my parents bought a house in Oxfordshire. It had nearly thirty bedrooms but they did not look on it as large. 'Large' to them meant a huge mansion with accommodation for house-parties. When my mother was a girl if anyone wished to have her to stay they were forced to put up five people—herself, father, mother, maid and valet. Our house, after children and servants had been provided for, had only six or seven spare rooms—a mere nothing, though more than enough for the thin trickle of relations which was all my parents thought it necessary to entertain.

My mother was not in the least daunted by having to furnish so many rooms from scratch. She liked shopping and those were days of affluence. My father was a soldier and in nearly a dozen years they had lived in nearly a dozen houses. As a result she had formulated various rules of furnishing which made it all very simple. One just went to Maples in the Tottenham Court Road or Hamptons near Trafalgar Square and bought whatever fitted in with the rules, naturally choosing everything of the best quality of its kind.

At any rate she did not have the nagging worry that the finished effect might not be admired by the neighbours. Both my parents lived in a world of their own and were indifferent to outside criticism. When my father was commanding officer of the Second Life Guards he used to bicycle to the barracks dressed in full equestrian panoply, and he fell in love with my mother because, regardless of the presence of a smart houseparty, she sprang out of a railway carriage and raced down the platform to buy a bun. (This dramatic scene is believed to have taken place at Oxford Station as, though eating between meals was usually frowned upon, we were always bought a bun-at-Oxford.) Happily eccentric when they felt like it, my parents did not care enough about art to want to deviate from the normal in their way of furnishing, and our Oxfordshire house turned out to be a 1911 period-piece, perfect in almost every detail.

Unobtrusiveness was now the ideal at which to aim. Anything that was noticeable was thought to be in bad taste. The saying that after a really well-dressed woman has left the room no one should be able to remember what she was wearing must surely have been invented by the new Georgians. When I admired the scarlet forehead-band of a pony in the Row my father, a man of few words, said, 'It's very vulgar'. Sad. I did like bright colours so much.

In other places, of course, other people were doing up their houses in other ways. As far

The Finest View in Europe. 'Snaffles' (1884–   )

The best-known sporting picture of the present century. It seems to be a law of nature that if you find one Snaffles in a house you always find several and that their owners when talking about them should become quite lyrical. The companion picture is *The Worst View in Europe*, '*Oh Murther! The dhrink died out of me and the wrong side of Bechers.*'

Snaffles writes:

The inspiration came to me during a glorious day with the Pytchley when my friend and patron, Taffy Walwyn, was an instructor at Weedon and he mounted me on his famous Rifle Grenade. To quote the authors of *The Irish R.M.*, it was just smelling Heaven, for in those days neither barbed wire nor tractors had invaded this fox-hunter's Elysium.

Those who possess copies of my first printing published pre-1914 will notice that the rider's hands are shown in the foreground, and that in the later impressions the hands are omitted—also less of the horse's neck is shown. The answer to this is that we used to sit back at our fences and the idea was to drive the horse at the obstacle, so of course the hands and reins would be in the picture; but with the introduction of the forward seat most of us were converted to that form of navigation and consequently the perspective was slightly altered, and the nearest object which came into view was the horse's neck and ears.

Old Arthur Nightingal suggested I did a companion to the *Finest View*, and told me how in 1901 he rode in the National on Grudon with two inches of snow on the ground which worried him and his trainer. However, they sent the stable lad into Aintree to get some butter which they rubbed into the frogs of Grudon's feet, and with the aid of a strong peg of whiskey he got round safely and won the race. But he told me that by the time they reached Bechers 'the drink had died out of him and he was the wrong side of it'.

as my mother was concerned, art nouveau might not have existed. It had never really caught on and now was dead and buried, only occasionally making a mummified appearance as a tortured tulip on a tile or on the cast-iron hood of a grate. Morris patterns, however, managed to survive and still had devotees. Somewhere there must have been arty-crafty vegetarians and simple-lifers with beards and bicycling breeches, drinking beer and laughing very loudly as they fought the losing battle against the Machine Age. Somewhere, to, frolicked the Mayfair intelligentsia, reading Maeterlinck,* patronizing the Russian ballet and Isadora Duncan and the Post-Impressionist Exhibition and getting their portraits done by Charles Shannon,who could be trusted to make them look like gipsy queens at the bottom of the sea.

Such people doubtless existed but we did not know them. My mother had no use for cranks and a particular dislike of anyone she suspected of being 'intense'. Our neighbours in Oxfordshire were retired generals/colonels/majors/captains and their families who had come there for the hunting and if they bought a picture it was probably a print of *The Finest View in Europe*.

★   ★   ★

Writing-tables are what I see when I think of my own home. We had a great many of them. Good visitors were supposed to write letters all the morning and they seldom wrote in armchairs because most fountain-pens unscrewed in the middle and were filled by a syringe and had to be repeatedly shaken and made blots. These writing-tables were kept in mint condition and they all had the light coming from the left and were supplied with everything that the most captious visitor could require, including a little glass pot with a silver mounted brush for moistening envelopes, and a paper-cutter supposed to be made of milk (we sucked the one in the hall until it became extremely sharp). All the equipment was bought at the same Sloane Street shop, except the tortoiseshell and silver set in the drawing-room which must have been a wedding-present.

The style that permeated the house was Hepplewhite crossed with Sheraton and the furniture was wonderfully well made, drawers running smoothly, cupboards opening quietly. The designs, even if not genealogically pure, were at least simple, the decoration hardly going beyond a narrow band of inlay round the edges. The general effect was that of a quiet, good-class hotel.

Wallpapers, cretonnes, curtains, cushions, carpets were patterned in nondescript colours. The roses had become so drab that they were hardly recognizable as flowers, and the fancy pheasants which now mingled with them were equally dingy. These patterns were supposed to have the virtue that they would 'go' everywhere, though curiously enough the flotsam and jetsam from that time which occasionally comes to the surface never really manages to match with anything. The curtains were beautifully thick, lined and interlined and bordered

*Maurice Maeterlinck, 1862–1949. High-faluting Belgian writer. His *Blue Bird of Happiness* was a household word, as well known in the nursery as *Puss in Boots*. His other works were chiefly about Souls and Death and Beauty.

with dog-tooth braid or silk cord, and every single window had a blind, dark blue or green upstairs, white in the drawing-room. Lace at the bottom was a bit villa-ish I think, but a silk tassel on the cord was correct, except upstairs where one had wooden acorns which could be unscrewed and lost. Fidgetting with the blind-cord was one of the ways in which idle children could be annoying, and they could also make an irritating rattle pulling the side strings—there were the blinds which flew up suddenly, the blinds that came down suddenly and the ones with several cords round swivels that were pulled up slowly like a creaking bucket.

Electric light had been installed when we bought the house and over every dressing-table, even the ones in the nursery storey, there was a pendant which pulled up and down. The shades were opaque glass—slightly waved edges in the superior rooms, though not too much waved, that would not have done at all. The bedside lamps had green jap-silk shades lined with white and with scalloped, pinked edges. The stems were brass—clubfooted for children, three legged for visitors.

The bathrooms, too, were up to date and the baths stood boldly out in the middle of the floor on Chippendale claws. Victorian baths had hugged the wall and were enclosed in a massive wood casing and luxury Edwardian baths had had any amount of taps and handles of uncertain purpose; our baths were very simple, designed for washing not fun.

Our lavatories had nice mahogany box seats and utterly efficient pull-up plugs and paper in yellow packets printed with a long rigmarole which every child thought excruciatingly funny, but were otherwise a trifle on the dull side. The real old-fashioned cosy-corner type had a blue and white china pan and a yellow glass plug handle, a carpet, the paper spread out in a fan on a fancy basket and kept down by a stone from the River Jordan, the archery volume of the *Badminton Library*, an old number of *Blackwood's Magazine*, and Kipling's *If* written in script and framed in passe-partout.

In every bedroom was a Japanese screen embroidered with coloured birds on a green background (silver cranes on dark blue for nursery floor). They had daisy-headed nails round the rims and mottled backs, and they must have been popular for a long time as one sees exactly the same screens in late Victorian photographs. They were very light and easy to move about and were most convenient for charades. Every bedroom also had a 'mahogany purdonium with brass fittings', a form of coal-scuttle invented, I believe, by a Mr. Purdon. On the rare occasions when one was conceded a fire in one's bedroom the *splendeurs* and *misères* were about equally balanced. Pleasant as it was to lie and watch the shadow of the fender flickering on the ceiling, the red glow soon got less and less and the shadows livelier and then one woke up suddenly in a muck-sweat as a coal fell into the grate.

The big stores stocked special servants' furniture and my mother, who liked her staff to be comfortable, bought for them strong, useful stuff though unfortunately of a horrid yellow colour euphemistically called satin-wood. The lady's maid had brown furniture to mark her unique status and the governess had real visitor's furniture (only her room was so cold that our last one struck and moved into a room vacated by a nursery-maid saying she would put up with a yellow wash-stand so long as she could face south.)

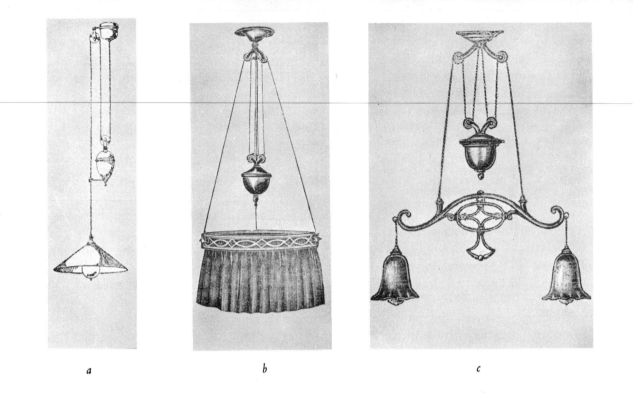

a	*b*	*c*

Lampshades from the Army & Navy Stores, 1911

a For the nursery.

b For the dining-room. It cast an agreeable glow on the table and left the rest of the room shrouded in mystery.

c For the best bedroom.

Just the sort of writing-table for a visitor's bedroom, though my mother would have considered the writing-materials very inadequate.   (*Maple & Co.*)

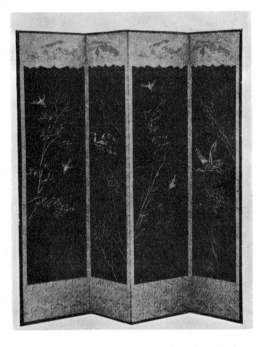

Japanese screen. Ubiquitous (*Maple & Co.*)

1814. J. L. E. Meissonier (1813–1891) (The Louvre)
Called *The Retreat from Moscow* for so long that it is changing its name to *1812*.

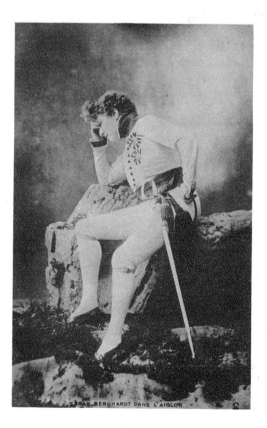

Sarah Bernhardt (1844–1923) in
L'Aiglon, 1900
The magic of her personality was such that she continued to take the part of the twenty-one-year-old Napoleon II in spite of advancing years and an artificial leg.

It was, indeed, a phenomenally cold house and was not made any warmer by the fact that the advantages of fresh air were a fairly recent discovery. Housemaids, nurses, governesses spent their time opening windows and airing rooms in spite of our burst chilblains and permanent colds—even the governess who wore a musquash coat during lessons had the same obsession. 'Don't be such a fresh-air fiend' was the only protest ever raised, and it had no effect on the window-openers as they were smugly conscious of being morally superior to the frowsts. The Victorians who hung curtains over their doors were despised for being 'stuffy'. So were the French Mademoiselles who objected to *courants d'air*. There were ventilators in the oddest places—and now one gets official circulars advising, practically commanding, one to block up cracks!

It was also a very clean, well-kept house, though the housemaids had few gadgets to help them beyond a jam jar of bees-wax and turpentine stirred by an old stick and a two-decker 'housemaid's box' containing all the paraphernalia for cleaning and black-leading grates. Tirelessly, they turned out the rooms in rotation, putting all the furniture into the passage and opening still more windows.

The difference between our London drawing-room and our Oxfordshire one was that the former was mid-Edwardian and that the latter very definitely belonged to the reign of George V. It was plainer, more English, more comfortable, and it was at its best when decorated with holly or when it was the background of a rollicking children's party. On ordinary occasions one was glad to edge out of it through the chilly hall with its grey, dull Meissoniers, imitation Turkey carpet and oak table groaning under the weight of assorted directories and into the less formal smoking-room.

This was furnished in a suitably masculine manner and became out of bounds on the rare occasions when a man came to stay. There was a knee-hole writing-table with a swivel chair and Jacobean-style patterned cretonnes and a machine-made tapestry screen and a big leather armchair where my father could smoke his cigar.

The smoking-room was also the library and I became well acquainted with the backs (though not the insides) of *Elizabeth and her German Garden* by Elizabeth, and *Elizabeth Visits America* by Elinor Glyn, *The Blue Lagoon* by H. de Vere Stacpoole, *When It Was Dark* by 'Guy Thorne', and the novels of A. C. and E. F. and R. H. Benson, W. J. Locke, E. Temple Thurston, Lucas Malet and Mrs. Alfred Sidgwick. I also recognized the stretch of pale green which represented the plays of Bernard Shaw. On the other hand, the plays of Edmond Rostand, bound in linen, were in my mother's sitting-room (or boudoir, as the servants preferred to call it). What fun we had reading *Cyrano* aloud! What contempt my mother had for the eagerly awaited *Chantecler*! And how I cried, up in the schoolroom by

Scene 5 from *A Trip to Melton Mowbray*, 1822
'And at his head a grass-green turf and at his heels a stone.' It was drawn by an amateur, a banker called Sir John Dean Paul, Bt. (1775–1852), and probably engraved by H. Alken.

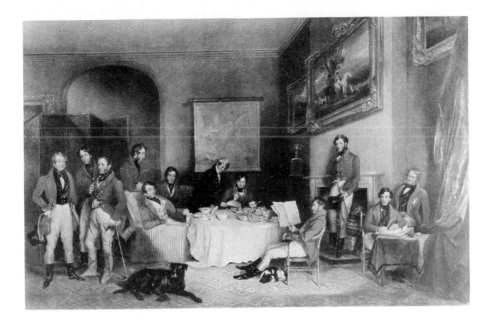

The Melton Breakfast, 1834. After Sir Francis Grant, P.R.A. (1803–1878)
Engraved by C. G. Lewis. From a print in the Victoria and Albert Museum.

The original painting is in the possession of the Earl of Cromer, descendant of Rowland Errington, Master of the Quorn Hounds, depicted (in a green coat) on the extreme right. The Duke of Rutland has a similar picture, smaller, and with two extra figures. Although the engraving has always been very well known, authorities differ absurdly as to which sportsman is which, how their names should be spelt and why the picture was painted. The following statements are therefore open to correction.

Left to right:

Massey Stanley, Esq., Earl of Wilton, Count Matuszevic, Lord Gardner, Walter Little Gilmour, Esq. (in armchair), Lyne Stephens, Esq., a footman, Sir Frederick Johnstone, Bart. (drinking tea), Lord Rokeby (with newspaper), Lord Forester, Lord Kinnaird, Rowland Errington, Esq., M.F.H.

The dining-room is that of a house at Melton Mowbray which was rented for the hunting season by the three men actually having breakfast. On the walls are a map of Leicestershire and pictures by J. Ferneley. The artist was a hunting man himself and would have known all the sitters personally.

When Grant painted Queen Victoria she described him as 'a very good-looking man, was a gentleman, spent all his fortune and now paints for money'. In fact, he was an ex-Harrovian, one of the younger sons of a Scotch laird, Grant of Kilgraston, and he decided to spend his patrimony on hunting in Leicestershire and collecting *objets d'art*, and then to make a second fortune at the Bar. The first of these ambitions was easy to achieve, but finding the law uncongenial and having had a dozen drawing lessons at the age of twelve, he abandoned it for art. The *Melton Breakfast* was his first Academy exhibit, and soon he was painting masterly hunting scenes, equestrian portraits and Society portraits generally. Eventually he became President of the Royal Academy, in which capacity he engineered the acquisition of Burlington House. His income was said to be nine thousand a year. And the best of it was that he had his cake and ate it for he never gave up his hunting establishment and when he died, it was at Melton Mowbray.

Red Indian. Ivan Mestrovic (1883–1962)
My mother had a weakness for the works of this
Yugo-Slav sculptor, perhaps because they some-
what resembled those of Rodin.

Hunt Breakfast. From *The Foxes' Frolic.*
Pictures by Harry B. Neilson. Verses by
Sir Francis Burnand. Published *c.* 1903 and
still in print.

The fourth and last scene of *The Midnight Steeplechase.* H. Alken, 1839
According to the *Sporting Review* of January
1839, the incident occurred in 1803 when some
cavalry officers quartered at Ipswich, arguing after
dinner about the merits of their horses, agreed to
race them immediately to Nacton church, four
and a half miles off. Lieut. Subden suggested that
night-clothes would look 'interesting'. ' "A most
original expedient," replied the Major, "whereby
we shall not only see each other better; but also
remain unknown to vulgar eyes, if any such behold us." '

The *Tatler* (1901), *Punch* (1841) and *The Strand Magazine* (1891) sometimes lay on the library table. They were all aces in their respective suits. My mother disapproved of the *Tatler* but she could not stop visitors from bringing it into the house and one term our governess tried to make her dull life more bearable by taking it in regularly. The feature I remember best was a series called *The Letters of Eve*, illustrated by 'Fish'. Eve was half-way between Anthony Hope's Dolly and A. P. Herbert's Topsy and she commented on current affairs and had a pekinese called Tou-tou.

Punch enjoyed a status which was nearly equal to that of *The Times*, although it was the fashion to say in the voice of one making a great discovery, 'I don't think *Punch* is as good as it was.'

The Strand was above criticism. It contained stories that were numerous, well illustrated, had a kick in the last paragraph and were guaranteed clean, and the whole family, including my mother, united to enjoy and discuss them. It was worth going the most tedious railway journey if one could bring home a new Archie or Bertie Wooster story, or perhaps a Sapper.

myself with the fire out, over *L'Aiglon!*

Also bound in linen were the Tauchnitz editions which my mother had managed to get through the customs. She was intensely honest, almost morbidly so, and would never have dreamt of smuggling anything else; Tauchnitz editions were her Achilles heel and smuggling them roused happy memories which went right back to her childhood.

A real old-fashioned country-house smoking-room would have looked very different from ours. It would have been shabby and untidy with grained woodwork (so laborious to do, so ugly when done). There might have been an illuminated address or two, and some battered looking sporting prints, perhaps by Leech, or that strip cartoon which begins mysteriously 'Solvitur acris hyems—it thaws—we must be off to Melton', and ends equally mysteriously at picture fourteen, 'Dulce domum—jamdudum animus est in patinis, exeunt in fumo'. And quite inevitably the four mad scenes of the *Midnight Steeplechase*. We had them in Ireland where they were hung so high that I could not read enough of the captions to find out who the men were or why they wanted to go riding in their nightcaps. The last one was just legible. 'The Finish—a Good Five Still Alive . . .—yah! yah! yah! Screaming and whooping like devil-rid maniacs they clattered through the quiet village— Cannon-ball first. . . .'

In our clean, tidy Oxfordshire smoking-room we only had one sporting print, *The Melton Breakfast*, and it was so neat and new-looking that I hardly recognized it as belonging to the genus. It hung over the mantelpiece and while my mother read Stanley Weyman aloud I used to gaze vaguely at it and wonder who the grave, suave, handsome gentlemen in dusky red could be, and why there were only three places laid at the table which was too small anyway, and not enough chairs. What had the greencoat said to the man on the right to make him stop writing his letter and look anxiously at the door? One could hardly imagine those God-like figures mingling with the all too human colonels and majors who congregated on the village green when there was a meet of the Heythrop. In fact, I doubted their intention of going hunting at all and suspected them of having come together for some obscure and nefarious purpose.

If it was really meant to be a hunt breakfast there was a much more convincing picture of such a scene in a book on the smoking-room table, *The Foxes' Frolic*. Although a non-rider, I had grown-up with hunting all round me, and I considered that the illustrator, Harry B. Neilson, had caught the real look of a hunt better than all other sporting artists put together. The accompanying doggerel was by Sir Francis Burnand, sometime editor of *Punch*, and was not very easy to read; in fact, I don't think I reached the end until after I was grown-up, when I discovered that the married M.F.H. had all the time been carrying on with pretty Miss Reynard in the blue side-saddle habit, which made the whole thing seem more lifelike still.

CHAPTER FOUR

Nurseries and Schoolrooms

❀❀❀❀❀❀❀❀❀❀❀❀❀❀❀❀❀❀❀❀❀❀❀❀❀❀❀❀❀❀❀❀❀❀❀❀❀❀❀

THE first real nursery furniture I ever saw was in 1915 when my grandfather died and some young cousins moved into the ancestral nursery bringing with them hygienic-shaped white cupboards with proverbs like 'Waste not, Want not' written on them in large blue letters. I was surprised and embarrassed—so insulting to the children to insinuate that they were not fit to use the same sort of cupboards as ordinary human beings!

Of course we had always had such specialized things as high-chairs and the baby's bath (round and solid like a Norman font), and the bassinette. As for cots, I can remember at least four. At my grandfather's it had been iron, painted green, with tin sides pierced by a pattern of tiny holes in imitation of some wickerwork prototype. I moved my eye from hole to hole, never despairing of eventually finding one through which I could see. It was irritating, and yet it was a cot with personality and charm. The cots in Ireland were massive wooden affairs, painted white, the sides filled in with willow-pattern cretonne that matched the night-nursery curtains. Light shone through the material in an agreeable way, and one could lie and ponder over the whimsicalities of the most famous pattern in the world. 'Three little men going to Dover, A weeping willow leaning over....'. It was crazy. The birds were bigger than the men and the tree had nothing on it but enormous catkins.

Later cots were just a cage of iron bars, white in London, black in Oxfordshire. But by that time I had been promoted to a small bed held together by brass knobs which could be unscrewed and dropped noisily on the floor. The brass made one's fingers taste disgusting afterwards, but the boredom of lying there with nothing to do was excruciating. One made stories out of the cracks in the ceiling and saw faces in the wallpaper and followed the ascent of the picture strings which increased in number as they went up the wall until they were six, eight, even ten strong when they ultimately met at the hook.

One's roving eye settled on the washstand. It was shiny brown wood and the top was brown spotty marble and the jugs and basins had a quiet dull pattern on them which, without acutely annoying, could not be said to give pleasure. The washstand we had in London was much more gay. It was white with a white marble top and it had bright pink tiles at the back as well as little shelves and brackets here and there and bows embossed wherever there was a bit of flat surface; and the rosebuds on the crockery were as pretty as anything. In Ireland the washstands were frankly Victorian, the classic sideboard shape with a basketwork shield hooked onto the back to protect the wall against splashes, and a sponge-basket (wicker or fancy wire) hung at the side. The kind of cover laid on it was graded according to the status of user—definitely American-cloth for children.

Illustration from *The Adventures of Two Dutch Dolls*—and a '*Golliwogg*', 1895. By Florence K. Upton (1873–1922). Words by Bertha Upton

l. to r. Golliwogg, Meg, Peggy, Sarah Jane, Weg, The Midget.

Florence Upton, who added a new word to the language, was born in America. Her parents were English. When she was sixteen her father, a business man, died suddenly, leaving his family very badly off but fortunately Florence was able to get work as an illustrator. A few years later she was inspired by some wooden dolls of the kind known as Dutch dolls (originally *Deutsch* dolls) to make a children's book, but she was held up for lack of a hero until an aunt produced an old nigger doll. At once she saw that he was just what she needed and his name came in a flash. 'I will call him Golliwogg,' she said.

The book made an immediate hit in spite of the lameness of the verses (contributed by her mother) and twelve more Golliwogg Books followed. Critics deplored the fact that 'anything so hideous should please and even fascinate children', but she wrote to a friend, 'The Golliwogg *is* ugly, but he has a good heart, and he is a dear fellow, and are not children ahead of adults in reading character? They see his beautiful personality.' Had she patented golliwoggs she might have become a millionaire; as it was she was able to keep her family in comfort for some time.

In 1917, passionately anxious to help the war, she gave the original golliwogg and the other dolls who had been her models and all her golliwogg drawings to be auctioned at Christie's in aid of the Red Cross. They fetched 450 guineas with which an ambulance was bought. The Foxhunt drawings are now in the London Museum while the dolls themselves are, eccentrically enough, at Chequers.

It is sad to have to add that Miss Upton was generally unhappy. Her ambition was to be a serious artist and she set up in London as a portrait painter, but though she had a knack of catching a likeness and some of her pictures had considerable charm, she was obviously not a great master. Noble, high-minded, generous and ready to worship, she was also over-sensitive and introspective, and she was frantically lonely until the last half-dozen years of her life when she developed a passion for automatic writing. Then, convinced that her dead mother was in communication with her, she suddenly became calm, friendly, sunny and contented, and she bore the painful illness from which she died with exemplary cheerfulness. Her grave is in Hampstead cemetery and on her tombstone it is recorded that she invented the Golliwogg.

30

By every washstand stood a matching china slop-pail; its handle was wicker, of course, to prevent a clank. At frequent intervals the visitors had hot water brought to them in a brass can; either a towel was draped symbolically across the top or it was covered by a flannel cosy which was more practical but always looked slightly squalid. Children had brown cans with 'Hot Water' printed on them. In some houses there were all-class white cans and my great-aunt had tall copper jugs from which came the delicious smell of her very soft well water.

★   ★   ★

When we visited other children we tried not to notice that they had linoleum in their nurseries. At home we had carpets; in London the cheerless, hard, old-fashioned kind that wears for ever; in Oxfordshire softer, more modern ones which were ugly in a different sort of way. The day-nursery carpet was covered by a drugget, and every week a man had to come and get the drugget out from under the furniture and nail down a clean one, using large nails with brass heads like sovereigns. Then the dirty drugget was put in a big hamper with the other washing and padlocked and sent over to our laundry in Ireland

★   ★   ★

Our toys in retrospect seem very amusing, especially the German ones. We had a German shadow theatre with silhouettes of people eating sausages, and a German magic lantern worked by paraffin, and a German toy swimming bath. When the war came, toys deteriorated noticeably, especially the dolls—English ones did not have separate fingers or joints at elbows and knees. On really wet days an improbable methylated cooker was produced and we, or perhaps our dynamic nurse, cooked a meat stew, dumplings and all.

In Ireland our toys included the Victorian relics of a previous generation. There was even a shabby wax doll that was so unattractive that I never could understand why, in old books, wax dolls were always referred to as the summit of desire. The rocking-horse was old-style black, on green up-and-down rockers. In England our rocking-horse was exactly the same as those which can still be bought at Hamleys—dappled grey and going backwards and forwards. It was considered the better ride. For one thing we could all get on it together; for another, it felt much safer.

When my eldest brother was tiny my mother wrote to a toyshop for the biggest golliwogg they had—golliwoggs were still a comparative novelty and nothing was too good for her firstborn. In due course a golliwogg 'the size of a man' arrived, which threw the firstborn, who was highly strung, into paroxysms of terror. So the golly I knew was only the size of a small child. Alas! nobody loved him. There was not a golliwogg addict among us, although we fell for a species of pixy-Buddha called Billikin, and grey animals, possibly badgers, called Billy Bos'n, and even were amused by peculiarly revolting cupid dolls called Pooksie. In the long run, however, teddy-bears got most affection and it is gratifying to know that in spite of pandas and other upstart rivals, teddy-bears are still undisputed masters of the soft-animal world.

One detail which has stuck in my memory is that on the inside of the lid of the cardboard boxes in which games arrived there was always, above the directions, a picture of the game

31

Fairies. Richard Doyle (1824–1883)

The same illustrations were used for William Allingham's poem *In Fairyland*, 1870, and Andrew Lang's story *The Princess Nobody*, 1884. Equally entrancing in another way is Richard Doyle's *Foreign Tour of Messrs Brown, Jones and Robinson.*

Lid of table-tennis set (Rottingdean Toy Museum)

Not quite the game-playing family I remember but near relations.

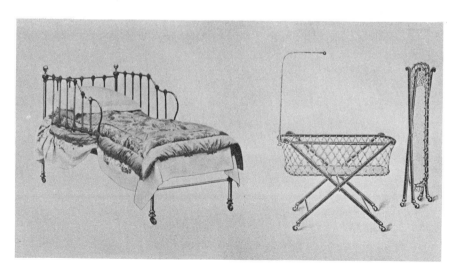

Child's bed (Maple and Co.)

Framework of baby's bassinette (Army and Navy Stores)

being played by a grinning family, a lady and gentleman in evening dress and a boy and a girl. They looked quite unlike any people I had ever seen, perhaps because they were wearing the fashions of ten years back, but they were drawn with such assurance and they appeared so often that one became convinced that somewhere they really existed, that family always in evening dress and always playing games in an ecstasy of delight.

The pride and joy of our Irish nursery was a large scrap-screen which had been made by my mother at a time when possessing children was an agreeable novelty to her. Although not in the top class artistically (really classy screens such as the screen made by the poet Byron, have small pictures arranged round a big one) it had been most efficiently varnished so that it neither grew blotchy nor peeled, and there were hundreds of scraps, most of which told a story—very good stories some of them, like the geese which saved Rome. Scattered about it were little Victorian fairies cut from Richard Doyle's Fairyland book. When we grew older we pretended to feel very shocked at this act of vandalism, but the pictures on the screen gave us so much pleasure that I now feel that it was justified.

Apart from the fairy book the main source of material must have been an enormous album of the Tate Gallery. In 1949 there was, at Burlington House, an exhibition of the purchases made with the Chantrey Bequest money, and lo and behold, there were the originals of many nice scraps from our screen. I am sorry to have to add that they put up a very poor show. At home in the nursery they had seemed fraught with interest; out in the open they looked feeble and wishy-washy. Anatomy and perspective were excellent but they lacked design. The colours were not strong enough for the large size of the canvas and neither were the ideas. One was led to the conclusion that the more of a story a picture has, the smaller it ought to be.

★   ★   ★

'You need pictures to keep down a wall-paper', was one of my mother's axioms, and our nursery wall-papers were given no chance to spring up. Every gap between the furniture was securely pinned in place.

The subject that occurred oftenest in our gallery was the Royal Family, perhaps as was natural after two coronations. Kings Edward VII and George V were only distinguishable from each other because one had a white beard and the other a brown, while Queens Alexandra and Mary were also extremely alike, hair solid as a pineapple and bodies armour-plated with jewellery. One wondered how their pearl chokers worked, whether they were strings of pearls wound round and round spirally or whether they were fixed to a collar which stood up by itself when taken off. Queen Victoria was much more alive than either of them, that is to say the Victoria of the Jubilee engraving with brown damp marks like the spots on the skin of an old woman. I did not connect her in any way with the girl holding a rose looking out of a maplewood frame with big calm eyes while her handsome Prince gazed across at her from the other side of the room.

An Empire's Homage was an imaginary view of George V standing in coronation robes surrounded by representatives of the Empire waving their flags and shouting. It was hung in a dark passage and was felt to be embarrassingly jingoistic, yet, let's face it, the Empire

33

Between Two Fires, 1892. F. D. Millet (1846–1912) (Tate Gallery)
The artist was an American and went down on the *Titanic*.

The Annunciation, 1892. Arthur Hacker,
R.A. (1858–1919).

Love Locked Out, 1890. Anna Lea
Merritt (1844–1930)
This must be a highly memorable picture, judging by the amount of people who have suggested that I should include it. The artist was an American and the first woman to have her work bought by the Chantrey Bequest.

CHANTREY PICTURES
AT THE TATE GALLERY

St. Martin-in-the-Fields, 1888. W. Logsdail
(1859–1944)

over which he was about to rule was truly enormous and would grow larger still. Next to it was a panorama of the Naval Review of 1911, several hundred ships, including thirty-two battleships. We also had *The Arming of the King* by Bernard Partridge, for many years top cartoonist of *Punch*. This time the King was shown clad in armour, and four massive women, Fortitude, Wisdom, Justice and Peace (I shall never forget them) handed him a variety of weapons. Speaking for myself the only royal picture I liked was an old calendar of Princess Mary and the five Princes and a dog on the deck of a yacht. The younger boys wore sailor suits like my own brothers and Princess Mary had the same Christian name as myself and though we hadn't a dog I should have liked to have had one, so altogether one felt very tied up with them.

After royalty, the next most frequent subject was peasants—not merry peasants, not cheerful *contadini* in bright odd costumes, not dance and Provençal song and sunburnt mirth, but poor and miserable peasants from the North of France and the Low Countries. It was always dismal weather and they wore thin, drab clothes, and the artist mainly responsible was Joseph Israels, a Dutch Jew who enjoyed a long and successful career painting the hard-working poor. I did not share my mother's penchant for them, in fact, I

Queen Alexandra

Queen Mary in 1902 when she was Princess of Wales

would much rather not have had to eat my cut from the joint and two veg. followed by puddings and pies in front of a family living on skilly with not even enough soup plates to go round.

Old masters were represented chiefly by Greuze (pretty girls) and Morland (scenes of rustic life mounted in black glass). The former I loved, the latter I loathed to such a degree that when, at the age of eleven, I joined with my sister in writing a book on art, I took the pseudonym A.H.O.M. for A Hater Of Morland. Living in the country myself I knew that village people, whatever else their vices, did not stand about in affected attitudes.

In Ireland some of our favourite pictures were coloured in that thick heavy way that was considered so marvellous when it was first invented but which was quickly superseded by better processes. These generally announced that they were plates given away free by *Pears Annual* 1902 or 3. *Alice in Wonderland*, a pretty little girl in pink brocade feeding a quantity of white rabbits in a sea of bluebells seemed to me almost as beautiful as it was possible to be and I also had a weakness for a teenager of later vintage who was sitting in a flowering may-tree and feeding a fawn. Underneath was a quotation from Wordsworth. 'Sweet childish days which were as long as twenty days are now.' The lilt was attractive though in our youthful folly we thought the words absolute nonsense—how could we guess the speed at which the time flies for those coming down the hill!

In Oxfordshire the visitors' rooms had been dealt with by framing a hundred or so sepia reproductions of old masters from the royal collections, but my mother had done her best to make the nursery pictures varied and amusing. The reproductions were of all sorts, historical, sentimental, domestic, landscape, and I never knew where the bulk of them came from till the other day when I looked through a pile of illustrated catalogues of the Royal Academy and found that practically all of the originals had been exhibited at Burlington House at some time or other. Old friend after old friend turned up, including

The Frugal Meal. Josef Israels (1824–1911) (Glasgow Art Gallery)

Blind Man's Buff, 1910. Arthur J. Elsley
He exhibited at the Academy from 1878 to
1915 and might at a stretch be called the Poor
Man's Renoir. Messrs Bovril distributed large
plates of this picture.

The Babes in the Wood. Fred Morgan (*c.* 1849–1927)
Another of Messrs Bovril's gift plates, and still cherished in at least one
London office. Fred Morgan surfaced surprisingly in 1963 when his
picture of Queen Alexandra with grandchildren and dogs (dogs by
Thomas Blinks) appeared in the *Royal Children* Exhibition at the Queen's
Gallery, Buckingham Palace. He began exhibiting at the age of sixteen
and was the son of Thomas Morgan who painted very similar pictures
including '*Don't 'ee tipty-toe*'.

The Railway Station (Paddington), 1862. W. P. Frith, R.A. (1819–1909)
(Royal Holloway College Picture Gallery, Egham)

A dealer paid £4,500 for this picture with its copyright, and a further £750 so that it should not be exhibited in the Academy. Engravings of it were once abundant but they are now hard to find. The group in the centre with the two boys going to school includes Frith himself and some of his twelve children. The foreigner having trouble with the cabby is his daughters' Italian tutor. Two real detectives posed for the top-hatted policemen on the right.

The Monarch of the Glen. Sir E. Landseer, R.A. (1802–1873). (Messrs John Dewar and Sons) Painted for the refreshment room of the House of Lords but the Commons refused to vote the money. It now appears as a whiskey advertisement and, consequently, is the only one of Landseer's stags which is still well known.

Coming Events Cast Their Shadows Before, or, *The Challenge*. 1844. Engraving after
Landseer
The original is in the possession of the Duke of Northumberland.

The Sanctuary. Engraving after Landseer
The original is at Balmoral.

The Stag at Bay, 1846. Engraving after Landseer
The original is in Dublin in the St. James's Gate premises of Messrs Guinness

Billy Bite's Scare-Cat.

Cats. Louis Wain (1860–1939). From *The Louis Wain Nursery Book*

'Wain first drew cats, of which he was a devotee, in 1883, and these became a few years later, the principal subject of his art . . . By the nineties his name had become a household word.' *D.N.B.* Poor Louis Wain was a case of the tragic clown. He was shattered by his wife's illness and death after only two years of marriage, and even at the height of his success, when he was turning out six hundred drawings a year, he was a melancholy man. To make the lean years worse he had sisters to support, and anxiety preyed on his mind to such an extent that in 1923 he was certified insane. In 1925 he was rescued by friends from a paupers' ward. A collection was made and an exhibition organized and he was moved to a more genial institution and given drawing materials. Ironically enough, his books are nowadays sought by collectors.

Peace, or, *A Little Child Shall Lead Them,* 1896. William Strutt (ob. 1915). (Brecon Cathedral)
There is a rather similar picture, also called Peace, which was painted by William Strutt in 1868.

The Piper of Dreams. Estella Canziani (1887–1964)
Though not, strictly speaking, a religious picture, *The Piper*
hung over many a child's bed as a sort of honorary guardian
angel. This reproduction does not do justice to his nice blue hat
and the robin on his boot and the primroses. The artist was a versatile Anglo-Italian whose interests ranged from folklore to
fencing and who during the 1914 war made medical models
and diagrams.

Vanity Fair, the lady in black velvet with the rose trees and the peacocks, whom we used to
admire so much. Apparently other people admired her also, as an almost identical picture
by the same artist (J. Young Hunter) had previously been bought by the Chantrey Bequest.
Also present was *The Pirates' Prize* by B. F. Gribble, who specialized in scenes on the decks
of sailing ships. Will the sulky little boy in the satin suit be made to walk the plank or will
the prayers of his mother soften the stony heart of the pirate captain? His face is a study.
One cannot tell which way he will decide.

Another delightful surprise was to find a picture which I had once glimpsed in a shop (the
art department of Boots, I think) and never forgotten. *For He Had Spoken Lightly of a
Woman's Name.* 'He' is bleeding on the ground and the hero stands above him with a rapier.
The artist was John A. Lomax, whose pictures of eighteenth-century life, *Fleeced, Rooked,
The Bitterness of Dawn*, and so on, can be recognized by the amount of things thrown on the
floor—cards, wineglasses, chairs, papers, people.

An even greater surprise was to find that Arthur J. Elsley had been a constant exhibitor
at the Royal Academy, although in 1905 the art critic of *The Spectator* had objected to his
'puppy pictures' being hung on the line. 'Why no protest from those Academicians who,
like Mr. Sargent, are true artists?' Arthur J. Elsley produced an untold number of pictures
of extremely pretty children with plump, smiling faces and perfectly lovely hair; regardless
of the silks and satins in which they are dressed, they romp merrily with puppies and
kittens. Another artist, Fred Morgan, painted practically the same faces, only his children
are generally in smocks and pinnies and play with old fishermen; sometimes, however, they
put on party frocks and then become indistinguishable from Arthur Elsley's. To be
absolutely honest, I wholeheartedly doted on these good and gleeful little girls and boys
doing whatever they liked in a land of pure delight, and I thought the titles like *Don't,
I'se Biggest*, and *Soft Persuasion* extremely apt and witty.

These nostalgic Academy catalogues also contained a great many pictures which I was
glad had *not* been chosen for us—sentimental mothers and children, farcical nudes and
allegorical scenes of such absurdity that it is difficult to put oneself back into the mind of a

generation which admired them. Still charming are unpretentious little sketches of scenes that chanced to please the artist's eye—tea in the garden, perhaps, or a dinner table by lamplight; but such things used to be considered trifling and low. In 1879 *The Spectator*, after damning the Academy and praising the newly opened *avant-garde* Grosvenor Gallery, rapped Tissot over the knuckles for being guilty of a picture of a lady pouring out tea for a 'couple of Hyde Park swells'. 'To have the power of painting almost perfectly anything in the world and to choose to paint a five-o'clock tea table!' This attitude was still prevalent when I was an art student in the nineteen thirties. One was supposed to be inspired by costermongers, Spanish gypsies, funfairs and circuses, while it was out of the question to draw a group of people in evening dress, a sight one beheld much more often.

★   ★   ★

When we ourselves went out to tea part of the fun was looking at the other children's pictures. Frith's *Railway Station* was in Mary and Cecily's hall. We never came to the end of the stories that it told, but we always started by picking out the policemen with the handcuffs. Barbara had *Stella Being Taught to Write by Swift**(lucky Stella) and also some Landseer engravings of stags. By that time Landseer was out-of-date and degraded and we used to make a ritual visit to see the stags where they were all jammed together in a little room. (Can it have been a bathroom or somewhere smaller still?) Nowadays, they have gone further and fared worse, except for the *Monarch of the Glen* which is familiar as an advertisement for whiskey and the original of which can still be seen by the curious if they peer through the door of Messrs Dewar in the Haymarket.

What other children often had, and we did not, was a comic picture. It was nearly always of nigger boys who were considered intensely humorous whatever they did, whether it was playing cricket with coconuts or being eaten by a crocodile. Or there might be some comic cats, fiendish ones by Louis Wain. *Everyone* knew Louis Wain's cats. And then in 1914 the taste of the public changed. His cats were not wanted and he sank into oblivion and misery.

★   ★   ★

I see that I have not mentioned any religious pictures. To tell the truth they were somewhat out of fashion. There had been such a surfeit of religiosity in the previous century that revulsion had set in and God was very much kept for Church. Raphael Madonnas slumped and there was a gap between those large, pale, repellent Victorian Arundel prints and the neat Medici reproductions which took their place.

We did, however, have *A Little Child Shall Lead Them*. My mother was privately of the opinion that the child resembled her first-born but I think we all identified ourselves with the youthful shepherd who was so successfully leading his heterogeneous flock, probably after a great many grown-ups had tried their hands at lion-taming and failed. Altogether a most gratifying picture and quite in keeping with the spirit of the Bible which consistently takes the line that children are superior to their elders, an attitude which the latter, in their obtuseness, have apparently never noticed, or else, in their dishonesty, have tacitly agreed to disregard, along with much else that is inconvenient in that awkward book.

*By Margaret Dicksee.

CHAPTER FIVE

Seaside Lodging Houses

❋❋

EVERY year we went to the seaside and after the restrictions of our usual life the freedom of the beach seemed like paradise. It was a novelty to be in a place which was neither town nor country, and the whole fortnight was such an exciting contrast to our existence at home that we even relished the repulsive interiors of the lodging-houses in which we stayed.

The typical seaside lodging-house was called something like *Sandringham* and was kept by a most disagreeable widow dressed in black with jet sparkling on her bosom and with a fuzzy roll of hair under a net. Embittered by years of struggle to keep her lodgers from bringing sand upstairs, she never attempted to fraternize with them, and as they started with the conviction that she was a shark, there was suspicion and hostility on both sides. Arriving hopefully, the eager eye beheld first the stained glass in the front door, behind which was a tiled lobby to act as strainer against buckets and spades and dead crabs, and then a very elaborate hatstand on which the mysterious other lodger, *the man*, had hung his panama. Beyond that rose a steep staircase covered with brown linoleum edged with key pattern.

The bedrooms yielded little of interest though we made the most of such novelties as there were, perhaps one curtain tied back with a string of beads and the other with a bootlace. There might be an illuminated text or two which we usually checked in our Bibles to make sure that they were not invented and possibly *The Light of the World*, a picture whose popularity is still undimmed. We studied this carefully, discussed the vexed question, 'If the lantern represents Conscience, ought it not to be *inside* the door?' and later went to inspect the original in Keble College, Oxford.

The bathroom and the lavatory (the plug only pulled if taken by surprise and in any case shook the house) were both extremely shabby and were papered with bluey-green Morris-style or art nouveau paper, up which ramped climbing broccoli or monstrous poppies. Why this should have been so I cannot imagine, but so it was, and in my mind I shall always associate Morris designs with plumbing.

On one occasion we were fortunate as the lavatory was en-livened by a picture, and such an interesting one, too. It illus-strated Campbell's poem about how Napoleon found on the

Marcus Stone, R.A. (1840–1921) in his studio in Melbury Road, London

Il y en a toujours un autre. (*A Prior Attachment.*) Marcus Stone
(Tate Gallery)

In Love, 1888. Marcus Stone

beach a British sailor, a prisoner of war, who was about to attempt to cross the Channel in a boat made from a barrel, and how Napoleon, touched by the boy's wish to see his aged mother, sped him on his way. The whole poem was printed underneath and although we did not mention the picture to each other owing to the place in which it was hung, we somehow discovered that, after a fortnight, we had all got it by heart. Even my mother (remarking, 'They don't tell stories like that about the Kaiser') chimed in with the last verse.

> Our sailor oft could scantily shift
> To find a dinner, plain and hearty;
> But *never* changed the coin and gift
> Of Bonaparté.

All this is rather by the way. It was the drawing-room that held the real treasures and which was the stereotype of hundreds of thousands of other rooms up and down the country from the best parlour of cottages to Harley Street waiting-rooms. It was, I suppose, a cheapened version of what had been fashionable once—possibly nothing less than Sandringham in Queen Alexandra's time.

In spite of a bright green carpet of a curious shade never seen nowadays, the predominant colour was a rich golden brown as recommended by cookery books. The hallmark of genteelness was a piano made of light blotchy wood, inlaid with squiggles and with squiggly candle holders and music rack. There was also a chiffonier with patches of engraved mirror set in the back and an overmantel with little shelves and pillars. Among the ledges a place was found for a clock in a glass case and a variety of vases and ornaments many of which have now risen in status and have graduated into the less particular antique shops. (Perhaps one day I shall meet again the looking-glass which I used to admire so much at Littlehampton. It was framed in velvet and there was an iris and two bluebirds painted on it.)

An aspidistra, quite unconscious that in most circles it was already a byword, occupied a bamboo plant-stand, and stuck in odd corners were some heather, some quaker-grass, and (in the case of very backward tribes) some bullrushes.

Heavy dark curtains were supplemented by curtains of thick Nottingham lace. I forget the name of the foreigner who, when asked his impression of England, said, 'Street after street of windows blocked by identical lace curtains'. Pulling aside the lace one could look out at a cloudy evening sky and the sea rolling in across the empty sands; Nature untamed.

Back in the drawing-room we had Art. There were sure to be some big brown (or possibly dirty green or chestnut coloured) pictures with a dent on the mount like an engraving and 'photo-

Her Mother's Voice. Sir W. Q. Orchardson
(Tate Gallery)

Napoleon on board H.M.S. 'Bellerophon'. Sir W. Q. Orchardson, R.A. (1835–1910)
(Tate Gallery, Chantrey Purchase 1880)

Orchardson admired **Napoleon** and the picture was intended as homage to a great man. The officers in the background are not his captors but portraits of his staff.

gravure' written proudly underneath. I never could see that it was anything to boast about as I would much rather have had an ordinary cheap photograph but they were considered very *recherché* and half way to a mezzotint—if one happened to like mezzotints. Besides these large photogravures there would be lots of other pictures of different kinds, among them the inevitable group of highland cattle. There might even be an oil painting of them. The craving for these animals had presumably started when Scotland first became fashionable, and though by my time they were objects of derision, they still turned up everywhere and we had some in our nurseries. Peter Graham, R.A., was the big name in Highland cattle but there must have been droves of minor artists churning them out. Other likely subjects were sheep in snow (J. Farquharson), birch trees by water (E. Parton or J. MacWhirter), landscape with trees (B. W. Leader), cows (T. S. Cooper), and stormy sea, rocky cliff and seagulls (various hands). There would also have been a costume drama by either G. Sheridan Knowles or E. Blair Leighton and, of course, a 'Dorothy picture', by which I mean a scene in which the chief figure is a young woman wearing vaguely period costume and obviously called Dorothy.

The period was indeed vague. The face and hair of Dorothys very definitely belonged to the end of the nineteenth century and they wore loose tea-gowns—no, not exactly tea-gowns as that would have meant sophistication and Dorothys were innocent to the point of idiocy; night-gowns is more the word to describe their dresses. For years I imagined that there really had been a time when girls went about dressed in nightgowns and big hats. Presumably it fitted in between the bustle decade and the coat and skirt days when my mother was young, and it was only after I had followed Victorian fashions carefully through old photograph albums that I discovered that the Dorothy period had never existed. Dorothy was just a day-dream of what love ought to be, a pretty girl sitting in a garden until an honourable proposal drops from the sky, which would be a perfect arrangement from the point of view of parents and men who wanted to settle down, and for the girls themselves at least one way of escaping from home.

If you went close up to a Dorothy picture the probability was that you would read beneath it the words, 'Painted by Marcus Stone, R.A.'. The name of Marcus Stone is not in the *Dictionary of National Biography*, though whether he has been omitted from ignorance or prejudice it is hard to say. He outlived his fame and when he died *The Times*, though kindly, summed him up as 'a lover of arts and cats, a devotee of fashionable attire and of his own elegance and refinement'. In his heyday this Dorothy artist had been a splendid, slightly truculent figure, one who had been called Marcus Apollo Belvedere Stone. 'A man of distinguished and pleasing presence and manner, a good talker, a clever phrase maker and an omnivorous reader. His memory was prodigious. . . . He was a militant radical both in politics and religion' and he often inveighed against God, the Royal Family and the Victorian prudery which caused him to paint such sentimental nonsense. 'One sells one's birthright', he used to say. He considered himself to be a kind of failure although from a worldly point of view he had made up for a bleak childhood. The son of an A.R.A. belonging to the literary and artistic world now called the Dickens Circle, he started exhibiting in the Academy at the age of eighteen, and after that, for fifty-eight years, he never missed

Dante and Beatrice. Henry Holiday (1839–1927)
(Walker Art Gallery, Liverpool)

Dante, having dissembled his love rather too well, is cut by Beatrice.

Henry Holiday was an earnest and successful artist, somewhat influenced by the Pre-Raphaelites. He worked in various mediums, including stained-glass. This picture was exhibited in the Grosvenor Gallery, 1883, and became a general favourite and it still figures among the small dioramas at Madame Tussaud. In his memoirs, Henry Holiday describes the trouble he took to get the details correct. As there was none of the old brick paving left in Florence he went to Siena where a little still remained, and he made models for the houses and statuettes of the girls—nude ones which he afterwards dressed.

Thursday. Walter Dendy Sadler (Tate Gallery)
The best-known 'monk' picture.

an exhibition and he claimed that he was always hung on the line and always sold his pictures in advance. Reproductions of his works 'were to be seen in every print-seller's shop window in Europe' and he was able to set up in a handsome house with a garden and a tapestry-hung studio in Melbury Road, Holland Park, where there was a colony of rich Academicians who housed themselves like film stars.

At first Marcus Stone had tried other styles. He illustrated several of Dickens' books and his early Academy pictures had names like *Stealing the Keys. It was already day. In sooth we were in sad plighte; our poor father a prisoner in his own house, the which was in the hands of the brutal Roundhead soldiery. No way was to free him, save by good fortune we mighte get the keys of his prison chamber before that the troopers should waken after their orgies. This my sister took upon herself to do, our good, faithful Margery quaking in the doorway.* People liked this, in fact *Stealing the Keys* went to the Sydney Gallery; however, tastes change, and in the later eighteen seventies Marcus Stone switched over to Dorothy pictures with quite short titles— *A Welcome Footstep, A Passing Cloud, The First Love Letter, The Proposal Accepted.* Reader, refrain from jeering. Did not Vermeer and Fragonard paint similar subjects and are not their names venerated by the highbrows?

Ironically enough, although Marcus Stone fell over backwards in his determination to make his anecdotes acceptable to the most straitlaced members of the public, the next generation thought his courting couples vulgar. My grandmother was quite happy to have in her dining-room *Il y en a toujours un autre* (bought in 1882 by the Chantrey Bequest) but my mother would not have hung it, except possibly in the housekeeper's room. I obscurely felt her disapprobation and wondered if the story was so very improper that it could only be recounted in French. The title was sometimes translated *A Prior Attachment* and as the man appeared to have a tonsure I suspected him of being the Prior who had the attachment, in which case it was certainly not a picture about which one should ask questions.

★   ★   ★

Marcus Stone naturally had a great many imitators, among them Maud Goodman who

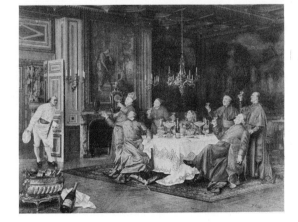

A la Santé du Chef, 1898. François Brunery The world's most famous 'Cardinal' picture and used as an advertisement by Messrs Moët et Chandon who have improved the left foreground. François Brunery was an Italian, born about 1850. He was middle-aged before he discovered his great talent for painting cardinals.

The Arab Hall in the house which Leighton built himself in Melbury Road, Kensington, and which is now open to the public. Photograph taken about 1896.

Flaming June, 1895. Frederic Lord Leighton, P.R.A. (1830–1896)
(Museo de Arte de Ponce, Puerto Rico)
One of Leighton's last pictures. It was lent to the Ashmolean Museum, Oxford, from 1915 to 1930, and when I was a child I was entranced by the orange dress and the sparkling green sea and the oleander. It crossed the Atlantic in 1963.

did sweet pretty Mammas with horrid little daughters wearing mob caps. Rather similar drawing-room scenes were painted by a Scot, Sir W. Q. Orchardson, but he must not be bracketed with the Dorothy Painters. He was different and better. For one thing he could distinguish Regency from *fin de siècle*. For another, his feathery brush strokes and pale autumnal colouring are agreeable. He also made gallant, though not always successful, efforts to design in the Japanese manner with figures balanced by blanks.

Fortunately for himself, Orchardson did not deviate very far from the conventional and having left Edinburgh and come to London, he flourished exceedingly. He had 'a distinguished appearance' and was a good talker and lived in a noble abode in Portland Place and collected Empire furniture, peculiar samples of which can be seen in several of his pictures. As for the wide, open spaces of his back-drawing-room, they are immortalized in *Her Mother's Voice*.

A more elevated note was struck by Henry Holiday's *Dante and Beatrice* which was very popular at the seaside, all among the antimacassers. But what about *Thursday* and the *Health of the Chef* and other pictures of good-time clerics such as the two in *Une Bonne Histoire* who were evidently considered so amusing that they were reproduced as china statuettes? Where did I see them other than on jig-saw puzzles? Not, I think, at *Sandringham;* the underlying sarcasm would have been unacceptable. Yet if not at *Sandringham*, where?

On the other hand, no lodging-house would have been complete without a scene of home life in Ancient Rome by either Leighton, Alma-Tadema or Poynter, three successful artists who were also exceptionally gifted men.

Leighton really had everything. He was wonderfully handsome, spoke many languages and dialects, and was extremely business-like. 'Punctual almost to a fault, tactful, energetic and equal to every social demand that could be made on him, he filled the office (of President of the Royal Academy) with extraordinary distinction.' His pictures were admired from the beginning, he could turn his hand to sculpture, he was a good and generous friend, he made a fortune, he led a blameless life; and the day before he died he was publicly honoured by being created a baron.

Alma-Tadema, a Dutchman who settled in England, had had to go through some early struggles and he was not a beauty. However, once he got started he went on and up. 'He was gifted with a genial and attractive personality' and 'his social success was rapid and complete.' He entertained largely and 'everybody who was anybody' came to see him. At one time he had a house overlooking Regent's Park but it grew too small for him so he left 'its Gothic Library, its gold drawing-room, its panelled Dutch room, its columned second drawing-room, with the onyx windows; its Pompeian studio, with frescoes from the Master's hand, its cheerful dining-room opening onto the garden, which ever in summer presented a wealth of poppies and sunflowers . . .' for an even grander residence in Grove End Road, St. John's Wood. This had formerly been the retreat where the artist Tissot had kept a mysterious consumptive lady and her little girl, and Alma-Tadema had to make a good many alterations and additions. Both his wife and the sister who lived with him painted, so there were studios for them as well as everything else. I used to know this house in the nineteen thirties when it was inhabited by another family of amusing individ-

September Morn, 1912 (Salon). Paul Chabas (1869–1937)
(Metropolitan Museum of Art. Anonymous gift. 1957)
'Il peignit de nombreuses études de ciel et d'eau, soit en
Bretagne, soit au bord du lac d'Anneçy, et, ayant eu
l'idée de les animer par une présence féminine, il trouva
la formule des Baigneuses qui firent sa réputation.
Dict. de Biog. Fr. Lib. Letouzey.

Alma-Tadema's House, 44 Grove End Road, St. John's Wood.
It has now been divided into flats and all around are rather
incoherent Roman remains, but 'Salve' can still be read
above the door.

At the Shrine of Venus, 1889. Sir Lawrence
Alma-Tadema, R.A., O.M. (1836–1912)
Sir Edward Poynter and many other
artists were painting very similar scenes of
Roman life. This is a typical Alma-
Tadema with plenty of marble and the
figures arranged round the edge in the
manner of a not-very-happy snapshot.

ualists and though it was very bizarre it was very likeable and, given plenty of servants, agreeable to live in.

The idea behind all Alma-Tadema's work was that people in the olden time were just ordinary folk like you and me, and he tried to bring back to life first the Merovingians, next the Ancient Egyptians, and then the Ancient Greeks and the Ancient Romans. Archaeology interested him and he took great pains to make his details absolutely accurate and though his figures remained firmly Victorian perhaps he intended that they should. At any rate, his patrons did not complain and not only was he knighted but he received the O.M. which, without wishing to be catty, one does feel was overdoing it.

Poynter, a quiet, modest man, of, needless to say, distinguished bearing, married one of the remarkable MacDonald sisters (another of whom married Burne Jones, while two others gave birth respectively to Rudyard Kipling and Stanley Baldwin). He exhibited at the Academy for fifty-nine years and was president for twenty-two of them, and was made a baronet. As regards money, he did not command such high prices as some of his contemporaries—a mere £3,000 for the *Queen of Sheba* is supposed to have been his high-water-mark. Still, an extremely successful career.

After reading about these painter-princes one hardly knows whether to laugh or cry, whether to congratulate them on the popularity they enjoyed in their lifetimes, or to lament that so much talent, skill, hard work and good intentions should be thrown away. Did a bad fairy come to all their christenings and curse them with some quality which cancelled out all their other wonderful gifts? Or should one see the situation as an allegorical group of the sort dear to our forbears, *Genius led astray by the Spirit of the Times?*

★   ★   ★

The Ancient Romans in these groups were usually fully draped, but even in the primmest houses one often found, sandwiched between *Sunset on the Nile* and *The Noonday Rest*, a nude. Sometimes one struck a whole roomful of nudes. *Honi soit qui mal y pense.* The people who owned them were not in the least embarrassed. Why should they have been? They had never heard of their subconscious selves nor of old debble Freud who invented two complexes for every one he pretended to take away, but they knew what was artistic. In the last century it was generally agreed that the Venus de Milo was the best statue in the world with the Venus de Medici and Apollo Belvedere second and third and the Laocöon highly commended; therefore if art was nude, nude was art.

By the time that I was taking notice the most ubiquitous nude had ceased to be the Venus de Milo and become *September Morn*, that is to say she was in the window of every picture shop. It was rather surprising that she enjoyed such popularity, as to some the idea of bathing so early in the day so late in the year might be less than attractive. Perhaps to her devotees she represented purity and innocence rising above everything. Be that as it may,

Mr. Somerset Maugham has recorded that when in 1916 he visited the red light district of Honolulu, *September Morn* was the most popular picture. And reproductions of it can still be bought in London, which is more than can be said for most of the works of art which I have mentioned.

CHAPTER SIX

Problem Pictures

✳✳

'EVERY summer at the Royal Academy', said my governess,* 'there was a problem picture. Crowds stood in front of it, speculating on the meaning. It was very amusing.' So my sister and I longed to go to the Royal Academy as we were sure we would guess the answer immediately.

Some of the problems were not exactly for the *jeune fille*, said my governess. There was often just a man and a woman and a title like *Disillusioned* which might mean all sorts of things. The best known problem pictures were painted by the Hon. John Collier and his most famous one, *The Cheat*, was fortunately of quite a wholesome subject. Four people are shown sitting round a card-table wearing expressions of indignation and dismay, and it is so wonderfully painted that you simply cannot tell which is the guilty person.

Alas! When we finally did get to the Academy it was a disappointment. The war had come and gone. Time had flowed on. Fashions had changed; and there was not a problem picture to be found. We looked up Collier in the index but he let us down. We would have compromised with one of his exciting historical scenes like *The Plague* (a man, having won his friend's wife at cards, calls to collect and finds her dead on the floor) but all he gave us was a straightforward portrait and an unambiguous odalisque.

However, eventually we were able to solve for ourselves the problem of *The Cheat*. Faded and skied, a reproduction was detected in a shop-window in New Oxford Street, and at once we were certain that we knew who dun it . . . after a moment becoming less certain.

Oddly enough, although everyone knew about Collier's problem pictures, reproductions of them were seldom seen. I suppose they were considered all right in a public gallery but 'unsuitable' for the home. My governess hinted that it was no wonder that Collier tended to paint questionable subjects. . . . She was not one of those who think artists and poets are exempted from behaving properly, and if people did not call on Collier, she felt that people were right. The funny thing was, she said, that for a painter Collier had started life in very tidy circumstances. His father, Lord Monkswell, had been a judge, and he went to Eton, a school which has a long record of *not* producing artists. Against this he married into the Huxleys, a family known to have funny ideas. Anyway, his wife, having exhibited in the Academy a picture called *The Sins of the Fathers* (not really the sort of thing one wants over the mantelpiece) expired, and a few years later Collier married her sister. He could not do this in England as at that time it was against the law, so they went to Norway where the

*Collective noun. There were ten of them.

55

The Cheat, 1905. The Hon. John Collier (1850–1934)
'The Man who practically created a description, if not a form of picture, cannot be called unimportant.'—
The Times.

Clytemnestra, 1914. Hon. John Collier
This picture became news in 1922 when
Blackpool Town Council considered buy-
ing it, and the London Press, ever ready to
make merry at the expense of the Provinces,
evolved the story that it was turned down,
not because of its size, but because the City
Fathers considered it 'wicked and nause-
ous'.

Mariage de Convenance, 1910. Hon. John Collier. (Cyfarthfa Museum, Merthyr Tydfil)
The details of the girl's bedroom are drawn with deadly accuracy.

The Prodigal Daughter, 1903.
John Collier

'The Prodigal Daughter is seen returning to her eminently respectable middle-
class home. Unlike the Prodigal Son
she is entirely unrepentant. Her old
mother is prepared to welcome her with
open arms. Her old father is made of
sterner stuff.'

A Fallen Idol, 1913. Hon. John Collier
(Auckland City Art Gallery)

It appears that even this picture is open to mis-
interpretation and Collier was asked to explain
it, which he did in clear, simple words. 'The
weeping woman is the fallen idol. It is a young
wife confessing to her middle-aged husband.
The husband is evidently a studious man, and
has possibly neglected her. At any rate, the
first thought that occurs to him is, "Was it my
fault?" I imagine he will forgive his wife.'

A Glass of wine with Caesar Borgia, 1893. John Collier
(Wolsey Art Gallery, Ipswich)

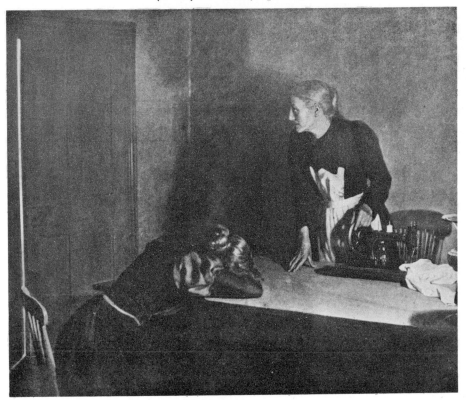

Trouble, 1898. John Collier

laws were Scandinavian. Naturally, this was considered a rather quaint way to go on and even after 1907 when the Deceased Wife's Sister Act was passed, people like his brother's wife, Lady Monkswell, were awkward about it.

Collier himself, a crusader for various liberal causes, must have thought the fuss ridiculous. 'A thin bearded man (he) gave the impression of quiet tenacity and a sort of polite ruthlessness', and on occasion he indicated that he considered the public extremely crass. Regarding the celebrated problem pictures, 'They are nothing of the kind,' he wrote impatiently. 'The only ones that have been so termed merely depict little tragedies of modern life, and I have always endeavoured to make their meaning perfectly plain. If I ever again paint a picture of modern life, which is doubtful, I shall give it a title a yard long, setting forth the life history of the characters, and, if necessary, their names and addresses . . .'

All the same, who had cheated? And how?

CHAPTER SEVEN

Portraits

✳✳✳

THE mothers of my friends were painted in white—sometimes full length standing out in the middle of a park in a white satin ball gown, sometimes just head and shoulders with a muslin fichu. The intention was to produce a modern version of a Romney, but the results were not dark enough to hang with the ancestors and the sitter invariably said that she couldn't bear it.

One rather agreed. Although mostly brides, the girls looked too old for their simple white dresses and pretty sashes, and their frizzy fringes and scraped back hair for some reason took away all character from their faces. The mothers of my friends had apparently all been exactly alike, with long necks, classical features, perfect complexions, full figures and an expression of lofty dignity.

These portraits were mainly by unknown artists, outsiders backed by the ignorant in the mad hope of picking a winner at a hundred to one. In the long run, however, it came to the same thing as if they had commissioned an academician. Portraits have to be very good before grandchildren want to keep them; also quite small.

Apart from price, the choice of portrait painter depended on the degree of splashiness required. At one end of the scale was the sort of picture that could be examined under a magnifying glass, at the other extreme the pictures-are-to-be-looked-at-not-to-be-smelt school. It was narrow-minded to think that it was only the moderns who had to be viewed from a distance. Lawrence and Raeburn had shown that a certain amount of splashiness could be very effective. Where did one draw the line?

The most famous and successful of the splashers was Sargent. He was in a class by himself. 'Oh well, *Sargent!*' Of course he did not really count as he had cheated by having American parents and being born in Florence and studying in Paris, so although he had lived in England since 1884 he had had an unfair advantage. And there was something else wrong with him as well, though it was difficult to put one's finger on what it was. He was an elderly bachelor who had devoted all his life to painting and lived quietly and inoffensively in Tite Street, Chelsea, but my mother made a shot at guessing his secret, and used to say argumentatively, 'I always maintain that Sargent has no soul', a theory that could not be proved or disproved and may have had something in it. However, in spite of this alleged deficiency his prestige remained high for many years, and is still higher than the pundits could wish; and really, when one compares him with the other society portraitists of the period he does seem rather exceptional.

Dame Ethel Smyth, composer. J. S. Sargent, R.A. (1856–1925)
(National Portrait Gallery)
Sargent was a devoted friend of Ethel Smyth's sister, Mrs.
Hunter, who presided over a literary and artistic salon at
Hill Hall, Epping.

The Chef. Sir William Orpen, R.A. (1878–1931)
(Diploma Gallery)
The Picture of the Year at the 1921 Academy. A firm
wished to reproduce it on bottle labels, the bottles to
contain 'one of the highest class products in the
Kingdom', but Orpen refused to consent.

Hazel, Lady Lavery. Sir John Lavery, R.A.
(1856–1941)
The beautiful Lady Lavery collected interesting men
around her, among them some of the Irish Leaders
who negotiated the Treaty of 1921.

None of the people I knew possessed a Sargent painting but I sometimes went into houses where there was a Sargent drawing, a big head done in charcoal with a blacked-in background. He was good at catching a lively expression or a typical movement and the families of the sitters were nearly always delighted with them.

Other splashy portraitists who come to mind are Orpen, Lavery, De László, Charles Sims and Ambrose McEvoy.

Orpen, an Irishman, was reckoned to come next to Sargent. His portraits can be recognized by the crosslights playing on the faces, causing them to glitter fiercely. To me the Peace Conference at Versailles will always mean Orpen's picture of it, but he made his biggest hit in 1921 with the portrait of the grill chef at the Paris Hotel, Chatham, in which the public discovered extraordinary significance. This was rather to the surprise of the artist who had got thoroughly bored with the tedious character of the sitter.

Lavery was another Irishman. The orphan son of an unsuccessful Belfast publican, his life reads like an improving story in Samuel Smiles's *Self Help*. With everything against him, he rose rapidly and was soon painting celebrities and living with the *beau monde*. His most permanent memorial is the colleen on the Irish paper money, for which his model was his second wife, Hazel, a lovely creature from Chicago.

De László, a Hungarian, also rose from obscure beginnings and soon became extremely fashionable. In spite of being hurriedly naturalized British he was somewhat under a cloud during the 1914–1918 war,* but in the twenties he shone forth brightly again and undoubtedly became top of his particular class. His sitters always looked very aristocratic, the ladies being swathed in vague veils in the vain hope of preventing the picture from dating, the past at that time being held in great contempt.

Charles Sims tossed together women and children in a bright pale light such as one might see on a sunny windy day at the seaside in April. He was Keeper of the Royal Academy Schools and though he fell foul of authority his ex-pupils are still devoted to his memory.

Less well known than the others, Ambrose McEvoy was almost rated highbrow. His misty and romantic looking ladies were to be found in charming drawing-rooms where the inhabitants were cultivated and enterprising.

★   ★   ★

Male portraits tended to be in such quiet good taste as to be invisible unless a quantity of them were massed together. In the upper reaches of country houses the route was often lined by lithographed heads of elderly gentlemen. Solemn and bearded, they were just bores, particularly as one had no clue to their identity. The words printed large beneath them all was merely 'Proof', and the few who had added their signature had scribbled a cipher which could only be decoded if you knew the answer beforehand.

Fathers in uniform were to be found in dining-rooms. Some of them looked so apologetic it seemed a shame that they had been forced into the army, and they were all greatly overshadowed by their wives and utterly extinguished by their children.

*It is darkly suggested that he was framed by jealous brother artists.

Mrs. Stephen de László, 1931. Philip de László (1869–1938) (P. de László, Esq.)
De László was the best-known society portrait painter of the twenties. He also did charming little domestic sketches.

The Hon. Mrs. Aubrey Herbert, 1917. Ambrose McEvoy, A.R.A. (1878–1927)
The Turkish coat is gold and crimson and the background is pale peacock colour.

Sarah and Diana Churchill, 1923. Charles Sims, R.A. (1873–1929). (H. R. H. Everest Esq.)
Sims was happiest painting dancing nymphs and fauns. When young he wrote, 'Be resolved that, if the work cannot be sincere, it shall at least be charming.' Eventually he found portrait commissions almost intolerable and turned to mystical abstractions. After his death six of these enigmatic paintings were exhibited at the 1929 Academy and caused great astonishment.

Most houses of any pretentions contained at least one monstrous portrait of a child. Led astray by the example of Sir Joshua (as Reynolds was affectionately called by the best people) these were often life-sized and full length, the girls in party frocks and the boys in Fauntleroy suits. On the other hand, the acknowledged ace of children's painters, Ralph Peacock, preferred to do children in their ordinary clothes. Realism was his speciality and he sometimes introduced a background of carved oak which looked so natural it was hard to believe that it was only paint. I remember that I had to touch the dress of one of his little girls in the Academy before I could believe that he had not stuck on a piece of tobralco. I wonder if the sitter still has the picture and if so, what it has been like to live with it.

The child portrait which everybody knew was *Bubbles* by Millais, whose fame was other-wise rather in the trough of the wave. The sitter was his grandson, Willie James, and he has never lived it down. Even as I write, the *Sunday Times*, after giving Admiral Sir William James's views on official secrecy, cannot refrain from adding that he sat at the age of five, etc. . . . The bubble was a specially made 'sphere of crystal'. Millais painted the picture for fun and then sold it to the *Illustrated London News* who sold it to Pears who added a cake of soap and distributed it everywhere. Pears advertised to such an extent that when I was a child I was barely conscious of any other advertisements (always excepting the enamel placard exclaiming, 'They come as a boon and a blessing to men, The Pickwick, the Owl and the Waverley pen', in front of which the Dublin train used to pause for what seemed

65

Ethel. Ralph Peacock (1869–1946)
Peacock was noted for his life-like child portraits.
He was also responsible for that curious fantasy of
a naked baby sitting on the edge of a cliff called,
'Out of the everywhere into here' (1904).

Bubbles. Sir J. E. Millais, Bt., P.R.A. (1829–1896)
For thirty years or so this little boy was all-pervading;
nevertheless, most people retained a sneaking fond-
ness for him.

The Artist's Mother. J. M. Whistler (1834–1903)
(Imperial War Museum)
Part of a famous portrait used as a poster in 1917.

like weeks). Millais was much abused for his vulgarity—by Marie Corelli among other people—though as he had already sold the copyright he made nothing out of the advertisements and was not in a position to take any steps about them.

By a natural association of ideas my thoughts turn to Whistler's *Mother*. Whistler had died before I was born and had become an old master, greatly respected although, like Sargent, he had rather unfairly been born an American. We were told about his wonderful picture and we very much longed to see it and at last a reproduction was discovered in some book. 'But,' we cried, 'it's *Old Age Must Come!*'

CHAPTER EIGHT

Old Ladies

✳❀✳

I HAVE the happiest memories of old ladies, from rich old Lady N., a childless widow, who lived with a paid companion in a house which overlooked Green Park and which was big enough to have a billiard room and who also rented from a Duke one of his minor seats, to little Miss D. who kept one maid and rode a bicycle. On the whole I preferred the un-married ones—they were more sympathetic and one did not feel that if it really came to the test they would vote with the other grown-ups out of *esprit de corps* and vested interest. Contrary to general belief, the spinsters who had taken to good works were particularly open-minded, unshockable in fact, as they were inured to skeletons in the cupboard and general irregularity. 'Just like my Robinson family!' they would laugh merrily after watch-ing Sarah Bernhardt in *Phèdre*. Their friends and families sent for them in times of trouble and they grew accustomed to crises and tensions, the sick, the dying and the dead—far more so than the hard-boiled novelists who kill off their characters like flies without, I suspect, ever having attended a death-bed or touched a corpse.

These quiet, unassuming people were ladies in the sense in which the word was under-stood before 1914—a luxury product, like the lilies of the field except that they dressed rather drably. They were entirely amateur and non-competitive and if they found them-selves making money they very well might think, like Charlotte M. Yonge, that the decent thing to do was to give it to charity. Manners and morals were certainly rather mixed and it was considered worse to be undignified than to be proud, but at their best they were positively saintlike in their unselfishness and I hope that some special compensation has been arranged in heaven for those kind, faded unmarrieds who would have been such wonderful wives if only they had had the opportunity.

It was not unusual to meet an elderly spinster who was very much liked by men and who seemed to know exactly how to deal with them; it seemed a mystery that she should still be single. The answer generally was that when she was young the fence round her had been too high. Perhaps she had lived in the country where, if one of the few young men available felt attracted by her, he could not get to know her better without the whole neighbourhood becoming aware that he was interested. As if natural circumstances were not deterrent enough, parents made things worse gratuitously. Although they believed that marriage was the only possible profession for their daughter they shut her up in what amounted to a tower surrounded by a briar hedge under the mistaken impression that a passing prince, driven to a frenzy of desire by the thought of so much purity, would force his way in with an offer. They were dragged home early from dances, made to refuse exciting invitations, and chaperoned as closely as though they were escapers from a reformatory. As a result the countryside was dotted with despairing Marianas in moated granges waiting for suitors who did not even know they existed, forbidden to do the smallest thing to attract an admirer or even to own up to what they were waiting for, helplessly feeling their youth and prettiness slipping away and eventually turning from anxious captive maidens into resigned old maids. A very old lady, the eldest of six un-married sisters, once told me that when she was a girl she had been invited to stay in Malta but she had not been allowed to go as her brother had said it would look as though she was trying to catch a husband. 'But would it have mattered what people thought' she ruefully added, 'if I had found somebody I liked?'

A further injustice was that it was assumed by almost everyone that until a girl was rescued by marriage she was her parents' chattel, and however brilliant or earnest she might be, it was her duty to grow grey at home, unpaid companion to a selfish, able-bodied pair who could do without her perfectly well if she had the excuse of a husband. Frantic with ennui and tingling with health and energy, these girls were forced to lead a life which was less active than that of many a septuagenarian. The married sisters were infinitely conde-

A PATHETIC APPEAL.

"Mamma, shall you let me go to the Wilkinsons' Ball, if they give one, this Winter?"   "No, Darling!"
(*A pause.*)
"You've been to a great many Balls, haven't you, Mamma?"
"Yes, Darling,—and I've seen the *folly* of them all."
(*Another pause.*)
"Mightn't I just see the folly of *one*, Mamma?"   [*A very long pause.*

Punch, 1874
This incident is too painful to be funny. The charming girl will go on sitting there beside her vampire mother and eventually die an old maid.

Queen Victoria, 1897. Woodcut by Sir William Nicholson, R.A. (1872–1949).

Selina, Dowager Countess of Longford, 1912.

Charley's Aunt, 1893–7. W. S. Penley, who created the part and played it for 1,466 performances.

Old Cockney, 1925. George Belcher (1875–1947). *Punch*

Belcher drew from live models and an elderly cook I knew was picked up by him in Harrods and induced to go and pose for him. After that she frequently abandoned the kitchen range for the model's throne, to the considerable inconvenience of her employer. Eventually her husband put his foot down because she had been depicted tête-à-tête with the local fishmonger.

Bonnet and Shawl, and how they fell into disrepute

scending and unhelpful to the daughter at home, though in the end their positions were often reversed and the spinster became the woman of the world who enjoyed shocking the sheltered wives with stories of life in Peru, Katmandu or Timbuktu (elderly spinsters travelled tremendously). Sometimes the improbable happened and, like the heroine of a magazine story, in middle age she found romance and all the bliss of an unexpected Indian summer. More often she could not make the jump; freedom came too late.

The classic description of old ladies is, of course, *Cranford*, written in 1850 and purporting to describe a distant past some twenty years before. My impression is that in my childhood the Hon. Mrs. Jamieson, fat and pompous, was still with us completely unchanged, while bicycles and Thomas Cook had helped the Miss Mattys to become much more independent. (Miss Matty was fifty-one when she tottered out to spend the day with her admirer, Mr. Holbrook, by which time her slightly older sister had already gone senile and died of old age.)

How old were the ladies whom I thought old? To my child's eye view they had passed some barrier and had reached a state where human emotions and physical changes had ceased to be. The rushing river of life had turned into a still lake in which they floated becalmed, quietly waiting for the final sudden submersion. If they said or did anything which suggested that they had ever been young or still had human hopes and desires, it seemed too droll for words. I never guessed that they resented the ageing of their treacherous bodies, some sadly resigned, others going down fighting; nor how forcibly they felt that, though let down by arms, legs, ears, eyes, heart, lungs, liver, memory, they themselves, the real them, remained as they had always been; nor how aggravating they found it when their own children pushed them off the stage just as they were beginning to settle down to their parts.

What *they* did not know was that they were living in a Golden Age. Old ladies had never had it so good and would never have it so good again. Except for wireless and air-travel, they had most of the luxuries that we now enjoy as well as excellent servants in endless supply. They were the last generation that could be *sure* of having a cook. Today, even in luxurious houses, one feels that to have secured a staff is an effort and an achievement. In the Golden Age a comfortably-off old lady could reckon on passing her declining years supported by half a dozen attendants in the house and a couple of gardeners outside. Best of all, when she grew feeble and ill there were plenty of hospital nurses who would come and look after her so that she could die peacefully among her lares and penates, cocking a snook, if she wished, at her immediate family.

In these easy circumstances any old lady with a modicum of egotism could turn the monotonous routine of her daily round into a sort of sacred ballet, herself the prima ballerina with a full supporting cast headed by an attentive butler as male lead. She never doubted that her act was beautiful and important and that the Almighty applauded the pomp with which she ate her solitary meals. In the morning she strolled round the garden; in the afternoon she went out for a drive and left cards; after dinner she sat bolt upright and read a library book; and then at bed-time there was quite a ceremony as the house was closed down for the night. . . . And so the time sped by.

71

Old lady's sitting-room. c. 1900

Note the text in the Oxford frame with crossed corners. The word 'Oxford' and the crosses combined to suggest high seriousness and these frames were seen on religious pictures, photographs of colleges, school groups and animal dramas. On the walls not shown there would probably have been a very small, very black oil painting of a blasted oak, a Bouguereau Madonna and *St. Augustine and St. Monica.*

Old ladies were generally quite interested to see the younger generation—so-and-so's children, dollies that could be put back into their box when they became a nuisance—and when we reached a presentable age my mother occasionally took us out to tea with elderly neighbours. There was nearly always something rewarding about the afternoon. For instance, at Colonel and Mrs. E.'s the revolting marrow jam in the cakes and sandwiches was more than compensated for by the stuffed bear in the hall holding a tray for visiting cards,* and the solitary Mrs. G. had a large landscape garden which was all the more fascinating for being overgrown. Temples and statues rose up out of the flowery hay like Maya remains buried in the jungle. She also had a bird which whistled *The Last Rose of Summer* which we thought embarrassingly appropriate as she was about fifty.

Although all old ladies did not have stuffed bears and gardens designed by William Kent, at least their rooms were *full*. The faded brown photographs, each one in a different kind of frame, were rather tedious but there was sure to be something one did not have at home, like a black firescreen with a mother-of-pearl lighthouse on it or (in the dining-room) a black oil-painting of dogs, wolves, lions, or bears killing or being killed by bears, lions, wolves or dogs; unless it was an equally gory painting of fish and game hung up for the attention of the scullery maid.

There was probably also a 'silver table' covered with curious knick-knacks. Lace was no longer an understood status symbol but everyone knew silver when they saw it. Even my nurse had a silver dressing-table set embossed with Reynolds' heads of angels, and my husband used to stay with a widow—a formidable one who insisted on white ties for dinner —who had so much silver in the drawing-room that every night at ten o'clock the butler came in to collect it and carry it off to the safe.

The older an old lady, the more likely she was to have parlour tricks, such as making cocked hats out of newspaper or paper boats from half-sheets of writing paper. (Their correspondents wrote on double sheets of grey 'silurian' paper which looked hairy but was slippery, and if there was a blank page they tore it off and kept it.) Some of them could do a few conjuring tricks and even the least accomplished possessed a watch which opened when you blew it. They knew extraordinary little rhymes and made swans out of apple peel, could take the lead in 'family coach', suggest forfeits, and the grimmest of our elderly relations one day sprung a surprise by beating us all at a face-pulling competition.

Some of them exercised their artistic and creative powers of dressing themselves in character and I remember meeting one dowager in almost complete fancy dress; she wore dove-grey from head to foot with a dove-grey poke bonnet and a long dove-grey, rather home-made-looking ear-trumpet. Most of them, however, could be put under one of two headings; those who wore bonnets and those who wore hats.

The former class modelled themselves on Queen Victoria; they were apt to be pyramid shaped and wore a top-knot of lace when they were indoors. One of my grandmothers, Granny, was a perfect specimen of this type; in fact I could not distinguish her photograph

*In some houses visiting cards were never cleared away and they piled up in a bowl in the hall like geological strata. In one stately home the pile received by a newly-arrived bride was topped by a piece of paper on which she had written the schoolgirl exclamation, 'Help!'

St. Augustine and St. Monica, 1846. Ary Scheffer
(1795–1858). (National Gallery)
At one time the works of this Dutch artist were considered peculiarly noble and sublime, and although his reputation slumped abruptly after his death, faded reproductions of St. Augustine and his mother could be found in old-fashioned houses until comparatively recently. It is only fair to Ary Scheffer to point out that the design is bold and effective.

The Virgin of Consolation. Adolphe William Bouguereau
(1825–1905). (Luxembourg Museum, Paris)
Another favourite with old ladies. Bouguereau dominated French art for a great many years and was the bogeyman of the Impressionists.

from that of the old Queen, and when she went driving in her carriage it was a ceremony as awful as royalty taking the air. I crouched on the little seat with back to the horses terrified of falling out at the sides, the only bright spot being a glimpse of the raven which was immured in a cage in Battersea Park. Granny was always muffled in black and her house was a dark cave chiefly remarkable for the number of small tables in it. After she died we lived there for a few months and did lessons in the back-drawing-room, the yellow brocade wallpaper being kept down by quantities and quantities of small steel engravings after old masters, Michelangelo and Guercino, Caravaggio, Carracci and Correggio, arms and legs, bosoms and thighs. My mother had moved out some of the tables and we counted those that were left and made it twenty-two.

My other grandmother, Grandmama, had been born a mere thirteen years later, but she had moved with the times and had got round to wearing a hat—rather a frightful one but still, a hat. She did not attempt to imitate Queen Victoria although she had actually known her and allowed no word of criticism to be spoken about her. (In most houses 'the Queen' was still sacred and when the anti-Victoria wave swept the country it was a great *surprise* to discover that she had ever been unpopular.)

Grandmama liked bright colours and wore grey and mauve and purple which was as far as she felt it was decent for a widow to go, and she was amused by novelty. When she talked about old days it was not to lament their passing but to relate an entertaining anecdote. She took an active part in forwarding causes that interested her and sat on the bench of a juvenile court.

Hers was a type which flourished in those days better than it would now, a type which seldom used their hands except for writing letters, hardly could tie up a parcel or do their own hair, certainly could not boil an egg; and yet were essentially practical. They could see at once what ought to be done and who should do it and they saved their energy for what interested them. Why keep a dog and bark yourself? was virtually their motto, though actually they never used coarse expressions of this sort unless they were in French.

Grandmama was literary rather than artistic and her pictures were valued by her because of their associations. In the spare bedroom (where the bookshelf contained Sir Walter Scott's disappointing *Demonology and Witchcraft*, Jean Ingelow's moving *Poems* and Ibsen's intriguing *Ghosts*) the pièce de résistance was the well-known *Infant Samuel* by James Sant. This prolific artist lived to be ninety-six and was Painter in Ordinary to Queen Victoria, but he has not got into the *Dictionary of National Biography* any more than Marcus Stone. He did many portraits, particularly of handsome, wide-eyed children, also subject pictures and landscapes. His romantic little scene, *Miss Martineau's Garden at Southwold*, was bought by the Chantrey bequest after his death and hangs in the Tate.

Downstairs in the drawing-room was a post-Pre-Raphaelite enamel of a saint and an angel encircled by some poetry which could not be read because the lettering was so arty and upside down. I don't think Grandmama cared for it very much, it was just something that had attached itself to her in the early nineteen hundreds. More conspicuously hung was a large dashing water-colour of her youngest daughter as a baby. They had taken a chance and commissioned a young Swede called Anders Zorn and it had turned out to

'*Speak; for thy servant heareth*', generally known as *The Infant Samuel*, 1853. James Sant, R.A. (1820–1916)
The companion picture was the Infant Timothy ('From a child thou hast known the holy scriptures.') but it was less popular, perhaps because Timothy was not nearly such a pretty little boy.

The Soul's Awakening, 1879. James Sant
Its companion is *Lead Kindly Light*. Although artists no longer paint people with eyes rolling heavenwards, photographers keep up the old tradition and this girl might be any modern actress in a tense scene. Indeed, films, having killed pictures which tell a story, now tell the same old stories themselves in the same old ways, and there is hardly an illustration in this book which could not be fitted into a modern film. Conversely, one can attribute Victorian artists to the latest stage or screen photographs.

be a lucky shot as he afterwards became famous. 'Died of drink poor fellow,' Grandmama used to say, regardless of the fact that he was still alive. On the stairs was an engraving of Lord Beaconsfield and in the dining-room water-colour landscapes by Grandmama's mother.

★   ★   ★

Everybody had a female relation who could do landscapes that were good enough to be framed. Figures were another matter. However, the drawing-rooms of old ladies whose forbears had been both well-born and artistically inclined often harboured a clutch of little smudgy child sketches by Louisa, Lady Waterford. These cherubs or *putti* wore indeterminate costume and there was not much anatomy but considerable chiaroscuro with an odd hint of Tintoretto. I used to think them unbearable soppy but now I find the sentiment charming. At least they are a genuine expression of strong feeling.

Louisa Stuart was the daughter of a diplomat, Lord Stuart de Rothesay, and she was born in the British Embassy in Paris. She and her sister Charlotte both grew up to be as good as they were beautiful. Louisa was really dazzlingly lovely, 'a stunner', Rossetti* called her and she was also gentle, imaginative, and devoted to painting. Her parents were related to half the peerage and she led the life of any girl in 'the best London Society' until the age of twenty-three or so, when Lord Waterford fell in love with her. Too shy to make his own proposal, he persuaded his sister to write to her mother. Lady Stuart was astounded.

Lord Waterford was notorious—wild even for those days. A street conjuror said of him '. . . His great delight was to make people drunk. . . . He was a good-hearted fellow was my Lord; if he played any tricks upon you, he'd always square it up. . . . I've seen him jump into an old woman's crockery-ware basket, while she was carrying it along, and smash everything. Sometimes he'd get seven or eight cabs and put a lot of fiddlers and musicians on the roofs, and fill 'em with anybody that liked, and then go off in procession round the streets, he driving the first cab as fast as he could and the bands playing as loud as possible. It's wonderful the games he'd be up to. But he always paid handsomely for whatever damage he did. If he swept all the glasses off a counter, there was the money to make 'em good again. Whenever I did any tricks for him, I took good care not to produce any apparatus that I cared for, or he'd be sure to smash it.'

Among the exploits attributed to Lord Waterford are putting a donkey in the bed of a stranger at an inn; painting the hooves of a parson's horse with aniseed and then hunting him with bloodhounds; asking the Irish railways to allow two engines to charge straight at each other—he would pay for the damage; shooting out the eyes of the family portraits at a house he had rented and sticking a cigar through the mouth of one of his own ancestors. He also betted that he would drive a vehicle down Rotten Row, sacred to riders, and won his bet by dressing up as a workman and driving a water-cart.

Lady Stuart was naturally going to send a refusal (her husband was in St. Petersburg) when she discovered that her sweet, fairly humourless daughter was 'interested'. Then

*Madox Brown persuaded Rossetti not to give Lady Waterford drawing lessons.

Louisa, Marchioness of Waterford (1818–1891). Painted in 1844 by
Sir Francis Grant, P.R.A.   (National Portrait Gallery)

Watercolour by Louisa, Marchioness of Waterford

followed some anxious months of indecision while London Society took sides. Lady Stuart could not believe that it would be for Loo's happiness to marry this barbarian with his 'boisterous, rough manners', while Lord Stuart and grandmama thought it too good a thing to miss (Lord Waterford was very rich). However, Louisa was left to make her own choice and as she had fallen in love and as she had detected a sweet, simple, joyous nature under the farouche exterior, she married him.

This incongruous pair got on perfectly together, the only blight being that they had no children. They lived in Ireland at Curraghmore, Co. Waterford, and he raced and hunted, and she had a free hand to do good to the poor and build cottages and make gardens and paint pictures. She visualized her husband as a sort of medieval knight and she read good books and the Bible aloud to him. He would return from hunting at ten at night and sleep for a couple of hours and then they would have a meal of tea, chicken and roast potatoes. Always she was anxious when he was out hunting and one day, after seventeen years of happiness, he was brought home dead, killed in a fall.

Louisa then left Ireland for ever, which must have had its compensations as they were troublous times and at one moment the house had been in a state of siege. She settled at Ford, a castle in Northumberland near Flodden Field, which Lord Waterford had left her with £10,000 a year. A rich, lonely, slightly bored widow, she occupied herself as best she could for the next thirty-two years, doing good works, building and rebuilding, looking after her property, painting non-stop. Among other enterprises she started a milk-bar to counter drunkenness and removed the strawberry gothic from her castle (oh dear!). In fact, she was the beau ideal of the Lady Bountiful, pious, graceful, in sweeping robes, always good, always kind, but sad. Her delightful sister who had married a politician, 'Clemency' Canning, and had lived very much in the bustle of the world, died in India, and when her mother also died she felt extremely lonely. She was now mistress of another large house, Highcliffe, the flamboyant chateau which her father had built on the Hampshire cliffs opposite the Isle of Wight, and which she really preferred to Ford though she tried to do her duty to both.

Her life was regular. Only once she went abroad—ten days in Florence. Occasionally she had a week or two in Claridges; very rarely paid a visit. Always the wolf at the door was loneliness and yet she could not face the discomforts of other people's houses and the hustle of general society. She suffered from depression. Was it worth it, she wondered, with no children to come after her, to spend so much time and money trying to preserve her two houses. Who cared, anyway? What were cousins and friends! 'I am utterly alone' she wailed in her letters.

Self-pitying she was, but not sour. The regrets she felt at the passing of her own beauty only made her more kindly towards girls who were young and pretty and going to balls. She even now and then gave a little dance for young people at which she was the only chaperone.

She drew children ceaselessly, plump, small angels living in Elysium. She painted after dinner by candlelight in the drawing-room, turning out sketches by the dozen and giving them to her friends, not deluded by their flattery into thinking herself a great artist.

'I see myself just an amateur and no more—not altogether bad but not good—no, not good at all; and it is the same with all amateurs."

When she was urged to live for art she replied stoutly that her duty was to look after the people on her two estates and that she was not a good enough artist for it to matter what she did, and anyway it was nonsense to pretend that art made the world better—look at the great artists of the past whose greatest works 'have not quelled evil, nor taught good'.

Sometimes her letters were extremely mid-Victorian. 'They say Lady Ruthven's prayers by her sister's bedside were most affecting and beautiful.' On other occasions she was the reverse of morbid. After enumerating various deaths among her acquaintance she candidly wrote: 'All this is very distressing but would be less bearable alone in cold rainy weather; there is no doubt that weather influences one though I don't think people like to own it.' Soon after her mother's death she wrote (referring to Highcliffe); 'Living amongst the shadows of all who are gone, in those great rooms, I can see father, mother, sister, brother-in-law, husband, and remember all are gone, and yet feel as young as ever, and (I must say it thankfully) as well and as strong, or stronger, than at Curraghmore where the climate did not agree with me, though I never owned it to myself.'

Her small circle of friends adored her and, to show their admiration, presented her with a life-sized statue of herself. And so, greatly revered and respected, she grew old and fat and died, leaving behind her in the drawing-rooms of other old ladies all those little water-colours of children, to be treasured by their sentimental owners, sneered at by the next generation, and by the present race of decorators to be remounted, reframed, rehung and revalued.

CHAPTER NINE

Little Folks and Others

❀✻❀

EVERY year we were given a bound volume of *Little Folks*, the children's magazine which ran from 1871 to 1933 and which was such a regular and delightful feature of Christmas that we never even noticed, much less resented, the babyish title. There were other annuals, of course, all welcome, particularly *Sunday* and *Chatterbox* which had first-class, copiously illustrated serials like *Jim Davis* and *Martin Hyde* by the poet Masefield. However, they were essentially old-fashioned and priggish and still smelt of the Victorian tunnel, while *Little Folks* had modernized itself, did not try to improve its readers and could be relied on not to mention religion. American *St. Nicholas*, whose dark red embossed cover belied its up-to-date sophisticated interior, had, it must be confessed, more punch than *Little Folks*, but it was a foreign luxury. *Little Folks* was a necessity.

We never saw it in its monthly parts and so we could not enter for the competitions (which otherwise, we were sure, we should have won), and as there were only six months bound up in one volume, what happened during the rest of the year was as much a mystery as the other side of the moon.

The serials were what really mattered, and their names still have glamour for me— 'Peggy D.O.', 'Round the World in an Aeroplane', 'Daisy, Dandy and the Duffer'.

Here before me lies a battered copy of the *Little Folks* of 1913, lent by a friend who has somehow managed to preserve it from her childhood. I could not have said in advance what it would contain, but as I turn the pages, each picture gives me a nostalgic thrill. Of the two serials, 'The Treasure Finders' has nice, unpretentious illustrations which have hardly dated in fifty years. The other, a Cavalier and Roundhead story, is illustrated by one of the Brocks. There were two of them and between them there was no costume from togas to gym tunics which they couldn't and didn't draw. They could do horses and carriages too and all their furniture is absolutely correct, but they were particularly strong on the Jane Austen period. Also present is the inevitable Gordon Browne, who was son of the Victorian illustrator 'Phiz' (Hablot Browne) and has been illustrating books since the eighteen seventies. Mabel Lucie Attwell has a coloured picture. Her chubby children used to be the mainstay of the picture-postcard counter; in fact, at one time if you wanted a humorous card not of the pier sort, a Mabel Lucie Attwell baby was the only alternative to a dog called Bonzo. Hassall is here too. He was a bold and clever poster artist—love him or loathe him one had to see him—and, when in non-facetious mood, a very good designer. Other old friends are the long-legged schoolgirls of Hilda Cowham and the leprechaun

1880   1913

Chatterbox. 1866–1948

1895

children of J. R. Monsell. And, of course, some Harry Rountrees. (He drew animals with a blotchy line as though he had a hair in his pen—you *must* remember his rabbits and mice advertising Mansion Polish and Cherry Blossom Boot Polish.)

Little Folks did not as a rule go in for arty illustrations but now and then there is a tail-piece showing a flicker of the pseudo art nouveau which used to turn up in children's books long after it had become the reverse of nouveau, though why children were supposed to like it I cannot imagine. I was always irritated by any drawing which might have been helping one to visualize the story and instead was mere decoration. Neither was I grateful for ornamented capital letters, presumably a legacy from the Gothic Revival.

★   ★   ★

Christmas also brought into the nursery large and beautiful gift books, some of them with the price, ten and six, inadequately rubbed out. We had two copies of *Grimm's Fairy Tales*, fat as a family Bible and illustrated by Arthur Rackham. One copy would have been more than enough. On the cover was the Goosegirl, combing her beautiful golden hair. Inside was horror and the cause of many a nightmare. Grim, we said, was indeed the word. Opinions differed as to which was worse, the pictures of ghastly incidents like the man who went into the witch's garden to steal rampion for his pregnant wife and, turning a corner, met the witch head on, or the ones where the danger is not yet revealed, like the sinister cat on the mediaeval roofs. The stories themselves, rough and rude peasant tales though they were, by comparison were almost tame.

Peter Pan in Kensington Gardens was also illustrated by Arthur Rackham. The pictures were pasted onto brown paper and covered with tissue paper and were all grouped together at the end of the book so one could not read round the pictures and to this day I have never found out why Peter Pan was drawn as a naked new-born babe when the statue in Kensington Gardens distinctly shows that he was a decent size and decently dressed. The gnarled trees with faces were fairly frightening, too, the gnomes were ugly, ugly, ugly, even the fairies were worn and jaded, and the grass was the colour of a parsnip.

But nowadays, when I see bare trees against the sky or snow in the Park on a late, cold afternoon, I say to myself with immense pleasure, Arthur Rackham!

Edmund Dulac, on the other hand, had our approval. This, I thought, is exactly what Morgiana looked like when she tipped the boiling oil onto the Forty Thieves. Fatima, too, and Beauty and the Beast, one would have known them anywhere. Afterwards Dulac took to drawing in a stiff, odd style which I regretted. I see now that he must have been looking at Persian miniatures but at the time I thought he was suffering from some sort of mental breakdown from which, I hoped, he would recover.

Other fairy books had equally beautiful shiny pictures expensively reproduced from water-colours. Among the artists I particularly liked was Frank Papé who was marvellous at doing the long hair so necessary to princesses—my generation may have been inhibited in some ways but at least we were able to regard woman's crowning glory with straight-forward admiration. Maud Tindal Atkinson also was strong on hair. She illustrated *Lady Anne's Fairytales*, a soulful volume written by one of Queen Mary's ladies-in-waiting.

Illustration by H. M. Brock (1875–1960). Only the real connoisseur would have been able to say, without looking at the signature, that it was not by C. E. Brock, 1870–1938.

Illustration by Gordon Browne (1858–1932). A prolific illustrator

JUST OFF

Illustration by Mabel Lucie Attwell (Mrs. Harold Earnshaw), 1879–1964)

Illustration by John Hassall (1868–1948). 'The King of the Hoardings.' Father of the writer, Christopher Hassall and the artist, Joan Hassall.

Illustration by J. R. Monsell (1877–1952)
Monsell's funny little people also abound in the pages of *The Children's Encyclopaedia*. This delightful Irishman was brought up in County Limerick in the house of his great-uncle, the poet Aubrey de Vere. He had no art training, his first book, *The Pink Knight*, being dashed off to amuse some children at a house-party. Extremely versatile, he drew and wrote in many different ways, and in 1935 his operetta based on Sheridan's *Rivals*, for which he had written the songs and music and designed the sets, was produced at the Embassy Theatre. In 1929 he married the writer Margaret Irwin and afterwards designed singularly effective jackets for her historical novels.

"There was an instant panic"

Illustration by Hilda Cowham (Mrs. Lander), 1873–
While still at school she began selling her drawings to magazines and soon became well known, exhibiting in the Academy and the Salon and holding one man shows, illustrating her own books and even designing a Hilda Cowham doll. Now, over ninety, a widow with failing eyesight, she writes with admirable contentment saying that her career was hard work but that she enjoyed it very much, and ending, 'I love cats and enjoy going out in the rain'.

Illustration by Arthur Rackham (1867–1939). *From* Peter
Pan in Kensington Gardens, 1907
Rackham loved Germany and his taste was for the
German Gothic. He made his name with his illustrations to Grimm's Fairy Tales in 1900. 'Although not
unappreciative of his material success he was modest,
cheerful and generous, and a methodical and business-
like man.' *D.N.B.*

Illustration by Frank C. Papé (ob. *c.* 1920). *From* The
Russian Story Book, 1916
This was the sort of Princess I liked.

*You SHALL go in, and take your place
among the Ladies you saw there!*

Illustration by Edmund Dulac (1882–1953). *From* The
Sleeping Beauty and Other Fairy Tales, 1910
Born French, naturalized British. Besides illustrating
books he painted portraits, and designed banknotes
and stamps for the Free French. He also designed the
Coronation stamp of 1937. This last was unfavourably
criticized by Epstein, and Dulac suggested that
Epstein should do a better.

Eleanor Fortescue Brickdale could be relied on to use nice bright Pre-Raphaelite reds and blues and greens, and her backgrounds were so circumstantial that one believed in them completely. Most entrancing of all were the intensely romantic, though perhaps not very well-drawn, illustrations of one Leighton Pearce in H. de Vere Stacpoole's gripping *Poppy-land*. When, in after years, I bought a second-hand copy, it lacked my favourite picture, *He Cannot Enter Here*, the one where a skull-headed figure with a scythe is trying to stop Gunhilde and little crippled Carl from going into the cemetery. Perhaps it had been torn out by its previous owner in a fit of terror; certainly when I read one of the stories, a robustly humorous yarn called 'The Great Bronze Tulip', to a young nephew, he woke up in the night screaming.

Roughly speaking, my taste in art was all for pretty colours and pretty faces and I may as well confess that I went out of my way to acquire *Hans Anderson* with pictures by Margaret Tarrant who, I thought, interpreted them to perfection.

We also had *Hans Anderson* illustrated by W. Heath Robinson, a comic artist not at his best with fairies and princesses. People still call elaborate, home-made machines 'Heath Robinson contraptions' but I have not seen one of his drawings for a long time. We were particularly fond of his book of war-time suggestions called *Hunlikely* (to begin with we wondered what *Hunli-kely* meant.)

Charles Robinson, his brother, drew in quite a different way. The nursery was full of his books from which I suppose that the grown-ups saw in him graces hidden from the young. From our point of view he had several bad vices, such as wasting the paper by filling it up with meaningless swirls and smoking candles and being able to draw only two children, a curly-haired one and a straight-haired one. On the other hand, that preposterous, absurd, snobbish and utterly absorbing book *The Secret Garden* (by the author of *Little Lord Fauntleroy*) still carries his pictures. Their haziness suits the craziness of the story and I should hate to see it illustrated by anyone else.

We suspected Charles Robinson of not reading the books properly. The person who really took trouble to get everything right was Honor C. Appleton, the illustrator of *Josephine and Her Dolls* by Mrs. Cradock. There were eleven books of Josephine and she had sixteen dolls, not counting the baby doll who appeared once and never again. In the first book (1915) one of them went to the war but after that current affairs played little part and Josephine seemed dateless and ageless until comparatively recently when the fact that she had both a nanny and a cook and did not go to school made her appear a bit old-world. I have read these books aloud countless times and I have never caught Honor C. Appleton making the smallest mistake.

In a different style, the Rider Haggard illustrations of Maurice Greiffenhagen, R.A., are everything they should be, while those in the Sherlock Holmes series are so utterly right that they might have grown spontaneously out of the stories without the assistance of an artist.

★ ★ ★

When I visualize the books which lay about on the nursery floor before I could read I see

Illustration by W. Heath Robinson (1872–1944). **From** *Hunlikely!, 1916*

'A quiet, shy, modest, and amiable man, who shunned all ostentation and liked best to live an equable family life . . .' *D.N.B.*

·DEDICATION·

TO JOYCE

Illustration by Charles Robinson (1870–1937). **From** *The Big Book of Fairy Tales, 1911*

Brother of W. Heath Robinson. He had great decorative talent and ornamented his pages in a very period way which appealed to grown-ups more than to children. He was also a little sinister like so many of the black-and-white artists who were contemporary with Aubrey Beardsley (1872–1898).

" Quacky dear, just think for a minute "

Above: *Illustration by Honor C. Appleton.* **From** *Josephine Keeps School* by Mrs. H. C. Cradock Ideal illustration. The Josephine series began in 1915 and, though reduced in size, it is still in print.

Right: *Illustration by L. Leslie Brooke (1862–1940)* From *Johnny Crow's Garden, 1903*

While the Elephant
Said something quite irrelevant

several that can still be bought today, such as *Struwwelpeter* (1847), *Johnny Crow's Garden* (1903) and *The Roly Poly Pudding* (1908). Although the Peter Rabbit books were still coming out, one felt as if they had been there for ever, and the authoress had no personal publicity so that when, some time in the 1930s, my artist brother-in-law conceived a great admiration for her art, we found that none of us had ever heard a thing about her. Finally our curiosity got the better of us and we rang up her publishers who politely told us that Beatrix Potter wrote under her real name and that she was definitely not the Beatrice Potter who married Sidney Webb and that she was still alive and that she lived in the Lake District. ('What did I tell you!' said my brother-in-law.) In 1943 Beatrix Potter died and a few years later her life story appeared, skillfully and sympathetically told by Margaret Lane. Our blood boiled as we read about how she was down-trodden by ultra-selfish Victorian parents in a big, dull London house in Bolton Gardens, and how her only escape was an occasional holiday in the Lakes, and how she amused herself in her seclusion by sending illustrated letters to the children of an ex-governess, and how no publisher would accept *Peter Rabbit* so she had to get it printed herself, and how annoyed her parents were when her books began to sell, and how, when she was nearly forty she fell in love with her publisher, only her parents opposed the match and the man died, and how when she was forty-seven she defied her parents again, this time successfully, and married a nice solicitor in Westmorland and became a breeder of mountain sheep and lived happily ever after. If her parents had been less outrageously tyrannical there probably would have been no Peter Rabbit books; and the moral of that is—well, it's obvious.

★   ★   ★

Beatrix Potter (1866–1943)

and they all fell to playing the game of catch-as-catch can,

till the gunpowder ran out at the heels of their boots.

Illustration by Walter Crane (1845–1915). *From* The Baby's Bouquet. The Old Man in Leather

Illustration by Randolph Caldecott (1846–1886)

PUNCH, OR THE LONDON CHARIVARI. [November 1, 1879.

THE HEIGHT OF ÆSTHETIC EXCLUSIVENESS.

Mamma. "Who are those extraordinary-looking Children?"
Effie. "The Cimabue Browns, Mamma. They're Æsthetic, you know!"
Mamma. "So I should imagine. Do you know them to speak to?"
Effie. "Oh dear no, Mamma—they're most exclusive. Why, they put out their Tongues at us if we only look at them!"

Illustration by Kate Greenaway. From *Under The Window*, 1879
Her Christmas cards and Valentines were already quite well known, but this was
the first book which she wrote and illustrated herself and it had an instantaneous
success.

Illustration by Kate Greenaway. From *Marigold Garden*, 1885
Her children had become much prettier and better drawn.

Also lying on the nursery floor I see the picture books of Walter Crane, Randolph
Caldecott and Kate Greenaway. By an odd coincidence these three illustrators were born
within a year of each other, and though not closely connected during their lives, in death
they are eternally intermingled on the children's book counter. I was never sure whether I
really liked them but they had a weird fascination. Who were these strange people and
where did they live? It was beyond me to figure out that why they seemed so queer was
that, however accurate their Georgian or Medieval clothes, they were not genuine but a
Victorian pastiche.

Kate Greenaway was perhaps the oddest. Inconsequent as her pictures were, her rhymes
were more cryptic still.

She was a small, plain, dumpy, quiet, amiable spinster who was born and bred in London
and the romance of her life was a Nottinghamshire farm where as a child she was sent on
long visits. Her father was a hack who engraved illustrations for magazines which was

fortunate, as it meant that she grew up to have a professional outlook and in other circumstances she might have remained a talented amateur like Lady Waterford. With her living to earn she naturally drew for the market and she made a small reputation for herself doing Christmas cards and valentines and odds and ends of illustrating. It was not till she was thirty-three that a publisher took a chance with *Under the Window*, a book of her own verses and pictures.

This was in the year 1879, just when there was a yearning to get away from the stiff and elaborate clothes which had been fashionable for fifty years and would continue to be so for another thirty. Pictures of Greek and Roman and pseudo-Regency maidens were all the rage, and so many women made efforts to dress aesthetically that they were guyed in *Punch* and in Gilbert's *Patience* (1881). Edmond de Goncourt recorded that he had been told that in England 'at nightfall, along the dusky roads, groups of young men and girls, dressed in the faded colours of the old-

Kate Greenaway (1846–1901)

world clothes brought back into fashion by the Pre-Raphaelite painters, indulge in flirtations interrupted every second by the rapid and silent passage of athletic youths mounted on velocipedes'.

Under the Window was an instant success and Kate Greenaway leapt to fame and fortune and during the next ten years she produced the books by which she is now remembered, making enough money to be able to move, with her parents and brother, to a nice little house in Hampstead, designed for her by Norman Shaw. She became a lion and was summoned to Buckingham Palace by the Empress Frederick, and she made various interesting friends. Of these the one who meant most to her was Ruskin, by this time about sixty but still full of enthusiasm and ready to tell her that the Christmas card she sent him was 'a greater thing than Raphael's *St. Caecilia*', as well as to urge her to give up the flimsy decorations she did so exceptionally well, and instead to make studies from the nude. Kate Greenaway had always adored clothes and in spite of her devotion to her mentor she continued to spend the evenings sewing picturesque costumes for her models. Perhaps this friendship helped her to forget that love had passed her by, and even after Ruskin was too ill to write his playful letters back, she continued to send him a stream of chatter about anything which she thought might amuse him.

'Did you ever in your life read one of George Meredith's novels?' (she wrote in 1895). 'It requires you to be in an angelic frame of mind or else it is that sort of worry—trying to make out what he means—for it isn't encouraging while he describes all his people laughing at a brilliant joke for you to be *unable* to see the drift of it. Whatever you do don't read *Lord Ormont and His Aminta*. It all comes of my being sentimental and romantic. The title was so lovely, but don't you be induced by any means to begin it.'

Although Kate Greenaway was only fifty-five when she died she had already outlived her popularity. The market had been glutted by imitators who shamelessly copied her formula. The eighties delighted in her and the nineties lost interest. Publishers no longer wanted her illustrations and she had to earn money by selling little water-colours and even by tackling life-sized oil portraits. She was ill and she worried about her income and she felt that she had not yet expressed something important that burnt within her. Cowslips and apple-blossom rejoiced her heart as much as when she was a child but she could not be reconciled to the ugliness and pain and grief that was also in the world. As for modern times, they were extremely distasteful to her, and one can only regard her death in 1901 as a happy release.

Moving from the nursery to the schoolroom I see the portly shape of the *Our Island Story* series—the older ones battered cream colour, the later ones smart navy blue. It appears that nobody has managed to write anything of the kind that is better and they are still in the shops, brought up-to-date and with, alas! new pictures. The pictures were what I used to like about them, particularly those by J. R. Skelton, bright, clear illustrations of people and places. This, I felt, is what I should have seen if I had been there at the time.

To tell the truth I never got much good from reading them. The print was big and plain but they were very long and every paragraph was packed with information—how could a poor child pick out the essentials from such a jungle of myth and anecdote?

The exception was the *English Literature*, which is the only book on English literature which ever made any impression on me. It was written by the same author as *Our Island Story*, H. E. Marshall, who suffered from the fixed idea that things are more interesting if they have happened a very long time ago. One was halfway through before one reached the two chapters on that pillar of English Literature, Sir Walter Raleigh, and I was so infuriated by the time I got to Milton that I wrote in the blank space opposite the picture of him dictating to his third wife, 'This is a very, very, very silly book fit only for donkeys.'

H. E. Marshall was also a patriotic Scot and was apt to trail his (or her?) coat aggressively, making such provocative statements as 'The 15th. of August 1771 was a lucky day for all the boys and girls and grown up people too of the English speaking race, for on that day Walter Scott was born in Edinburgh'. He (or she?) should have seen the fuss my brother made when he got *Old Mortality* for a holiday task! Scott, I decided, was a smug prig. So were Sir Thomas More, Wordsworth, Carlyle, and above all, Addison. 'See how a Christian can die!' indeed. Conceited beast. Give me Byron every time.

All the same, H. E. Marshall has won. I mocked and fumed but I have not forgotten. I cannot get it out of my head that the English writers who really matter are Caedmon, Skelton, Dunbar, and James I of Scotland, and that as no mention was made of Donne, Fielding, Jane Austen, the Brontes, or Browning,* they must be pretty second-rate.

*Only four Victorians qualify. The Four Just Men are Tennyson, Dickens, Thackeray and, of course, Carlyle.

Another all-pervading pedagogue was Arthur Mee, a journalist who had been successful from his earliest years and who edited and wrote a great number of semi-educational books, among them the *Children's Encyclopaedia* (1908). This became a classic and was continued as a monthly magazine under the witty, though possibly annoying, name of *My Magazine*. An inexhaustible bran-tub, it had its attraction, but its complacent mixture of science and religion drove us hopping mad. We used to make up parodies of the captions exhorting us to admire something or other, on the lines of 'The Cobbler Who Cooked a King' (those low-church cobblers were always being tiresome). We grew to hate the word science. Science is miraculous! Science is sacred! Bow down and worship science for science is shortly going to rule the world and then will come the era of universal joy and the brotherhood of man!

Nowadays people talk about science in quite a different voice, a humble, frightened voice. . . .

Illustration by Sidney Paget (1860–1908). From The Hound of the Baskervilles, *1902*
Few people remember the name of Sidney Paget, although he illustrated the Sherlock Holmes stories when they first appeared in the *Strand Magazine* and so fixed for ever the appearance of the great detective.

CHAPTER TEN

Soldiers

✳✳✳

WHEREVER we were, England or Ireland, London or country, there was one constant feature in the background of our lives. Our father was a soldier, and I assumed that should I ever succeed in becoming a grown-up, I too would go into the Cavalry (though not, of course, sacrificing my hair which by that time would have become black as ebony and reach to the ground).

Anyone could see that men had more fun than women so it was obvious that when one was captain of one's fate one would choose the better life, and had I been given the choice I would have opted right away to be a boy. In our family the pecking-order worked on the crude principle that boys were more valuable than girls (though only the grandmother of the clan could have told whether the son of a daughter rated higher than the daughter of a son). Eldest sons were invested with a peculiar sanctity but I did not envy them their pomp and circumstance; to be a simple soldier of fortune was all I asked.

I might have seen the matter differently if my female relations had been smart and vain and had dolled themselves up in gorgeous array, but they timidly dressed in shades of mud and it was my father, indifferent as he was to his appearance, who in effect wore the fine feathers. He went out hunting in a red coat and the house was dotted with photographs of him in the splendiferous uniform of the Life Guards. By the time I can remember, his men had become Yeomanry, but we never saw the Yeomandry (sic) and we were often granted a vision of Life Guards, two and two on their black chargers serenely proceeding on their glorious way above the dingy muddle of traffic. If they had white hearthrugs under their saddles they were *our* ones, the Second. The First (whom one would have expected to be superior but were really inferior) had black hearthrugs. Both were better than the Blues who aped our uniform so that one often mistook them for Life Guards until one noticed their blue sleeves and red plumes. Sometimes, early in the morning, we would hear the clipper-clop of many horses and my sister and I would spring out of bed and crane out of the window to see a cavalcade passing at the end of the Square. As they were then in négligé without distinguishing features one could assume they were the right sort and occasionally they proved it by turning the corner and coming past our house.

My brothers had large tin armies which we played with on the floor and I even had a mounted detachment myself—five Arabs and an officer in a bearskin. My father's soldiers had the advantage that they were real. There was talk of manœuvres and sham fights and cavalry charges, and he told me that when I was born he did not see me until I was two days

My father considered that his clothes were his own affair, and many stories were told about the eccentricity of his dress.

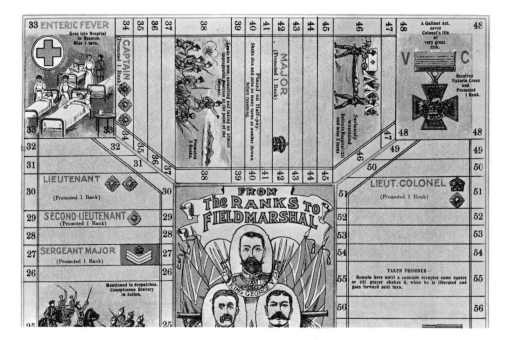

Children's dice game, c. 1914

old as he was encamped at Uffington beneath the White Horse Hill. He also told me never to sit down to a meal till I had seen that my men and my horses were fed and never to wear pink at a hunt ball. Now and then when he came to say good-night to us he was going to a military dinner—which one pictured as a gorgeous banquet—and wore medals which clanked and glittered in the darkness, and when we pulled his shirt open we could see the coat of arms which had been tattooed on his chest so that his corpse could be recognized on the field of battle, like the pictures of Harold at Hastings. (The way things turned out he was posted wounded and missing in Gallipoli and his body was never found.)

We assumed that patriotism was one of the basic virtues, like courage, truth or unselfishness.

There has been so much debunking in the last fifty years that it is an effort to remember how delightfully simple world affairs used to look—the whites so white and the blacks so black and England always in the right. Many moons passed before my elder brother revealed to the schoolroom that England had been wrong in *all* her wars. Later still, my eldest sister, doing the London season, reported back that *all* soldiers were halfwitted. But ignorance is sometimes bliss and I had no uncomfortable doubts when I took to my heart Gideon and Alexander and Richard Coeur de Lion, and the whole family had shares in a semi-mythical great uncle by marriage who had been taken prisoner at the Charge of the Light Brigade and had escaped on a runaway horse, to our eternal credit.

Having no television and seldom seeing a cinema we worked off our natural savage instincts by bellowing blood-thirsty poetry, of which we knew a great deal. That we should learn poetry by heart was regarded as a necessity, like French verbs, or *bijou, caillou, chou, genou, hibou, joujou, POU*, and we memorized a good deal of Newbolt. How pleasant it was to sit on a gate among the sleepy summer fields and shout, 'The Gatling's jammed and the Colonel's dead', or 'If the Dons sight Devon I'll quit the port of Heaven', or the goosefleshy ' "Ye have robbed', he said,"ye have slaughtered and made an end." '

There was also Macaulay and Scott and Aytoun ('And the evening star was shining. On Schiehallion's distant head, When we wiped our bloody broadswords, And returned to count the dead.') not to mention John Greenleaf Whittier ('And the tartan clove the turban As the Goomtee cleaves the plain.').

Do not imagine that we were so unsophisticated that we uncritically accepted just any old thing. Many famous poems had already sunk to the position of school jokes, and stories which were intrinsically heroic and which would be very moving as a short sequence in a film had become so hackneyed as to seem ludicrous. Time-honoured *Casabianca* (by Mrs. Hemans, authoress of *The Stately Homes of England*) we only knew through its parodies such as 'The boy stood on the railway line', or 'in the dining-room', and I never found out whether Casabianca was his name, or the name of his ship, or the spot where the accident occurred. *The Private of the Buffs* by Sir Francis Doyle had also been downgraded from the sublime to the ridiculous.

> Last night, among his fellow roughs
> He jested quaffed and swore,
> A drunken private of the Buffs,

Who never looked before.
Today . . .

The story as told by the China correspondent of *The Times* was that

Some Seiks, and a private of the Buffs, having remained behind with the grog-carts, fell into the hands of the Chinese. On the next morning they were brought before the authorities, and commanded to perform the Kotou. The Seiks obeyed; but Moyse, the English soldier, declaring that he would not prostrate himself before any Chinaman alive, was immediately knocked upon the head, and his body thrown on a dunghill.

Modern research had revealed that poor Moyse, far from being a Kentish lad, was a Scot aged thirty-two who was a private because he had been reduced from the rank of colour sergeant for insubordinate language. All the same, it seems unfair to call him drunken just because he was in charge of the grog carts.

The Red Thread of Honour, also by Sir Francis Doyle, seemed to have worn better and many of the lines have stuck in my head.

Eleven men of England,
A breastwork charged in vain;
Eleven men of England,
Lie stripped, and gashed, and slain.

The eleven English soldiers had made a mad attack on a hill fort and their opponents, to mark their admiration, tied red threads, the highest possible honour, round the wrists of the dead.

The songs they sing of Roostrum
Fill all the past with light;
If truth be in their music,
He was a noble knight.
But were those heroes living,
And strong for battle still,
Would Mehrab Khan or Roostrum
Have climbed, like these, the Hill?

Eventually news of it reached the English general.

Thus Napier's knightly heart, touched to the core,
Rung like an echo, to that knightly deed,
He bade its memory live for everymore
That those who run may read.

Kipling was still very much alive in all senses of the word, and although he was sticky about allowing his poems to appear in anthologies they percolated through to us somehow. My childhood would have been the poorer without 'Kamal is out with twenty men to raise the border side'. Kipling was easy to learn and splendid to shout, and it was one of the mysteries of the world why he had not been made Poet Laureate instead of old buffer Bridges. My governess explained in a low voice that Kipling had written things 'against the Government' which sounded bad, but perhaps no more than one would expect from someone whose *History of England* was too slangy to be used in the schoolroom. (By mutual consent we closed its pages when he called the barons 'rowdies'.) I was always a little puzzled by the attitude of the grown-ups towards Kipling; they obviously admired him tremendously and yet seemed nervous about how he would behave. Apparently he was one of those embarrassing people who tell you the low-down in confidence but in much too loud a voice.

★   ★   ★

I suppose we all read to escape, and when I visualize the ladylike sitting-rooms of my mother and her friends I see, lying on an occasional table, the slim blue volumes of Robert Service, the Canadian Kipling, who was supposed to have made a six-figure fortune out of his verse. They were called things like *Songs of a Sourdough*, and as I did not know what a sourdough was and as Service was rather a noble, religious sort of word, I pictured the author as one of those army padres whose booklets were popular during the war. No one suggested that we should learn these poems by heart, or even gave us a chance to read them. However, everything comes to him who waits, and eventually I was taken to a village concert in Wales where I heard the dramatic recitation that begins:

A bunch of the boys were whooping it up in the Mulamute saloon;
The kid that handles the music box was hitting a rag-time tune;
Back of the bar, in a solo game, sat Dangerous Dan Magrew,
And watching his luck was his light-o-love, the lady that's known as Lou.

So that's what my Mamma and Aunt Cynthia were reading!

★   ★   ★

As for pictures of battles, there were plenty of them in our history books. Swords flashed, arrows flew, corpses strewed the ground. One cannot help admiring the accomplishment of the artists who turned out these complicated scenes of struggling men and horses, especially the ones who produced them quickly for the newspapers.

We were not at all averse to having an occasional battlepiece on the walls. My brother at Eton had the one always referred to as *The Cavalry Charge* (I never heard who painted it) which was held in such respect that the story that an American looked at it and asked, 'What was after them?' shocked and amused like blasphemy; and in the bedroom I shared with my sister there hung over the mantelpiece a drawing, which she had cut out of *The Illustrated London News*, of Captain Loxley going down on the *Formidable*, his dog beside him—when I think of that trusting little terrier I can hardly keep from crying, even now. Still, we were rather at the end of a period. News photography was improving and the great days of battle illustration had been in the previous century. It is true that Lady Butler was still alive and painting, but she was a relic of another age, and the engraving we had of her famous *Roll-Call* was hung in that place of banishment, the wing. Our governess told us how, when it was first shown at the Academy, Lady Butler became famous in a night, and I wondered if such a thing could ever happen to me. The answer was no, not if I painted ever so. People are different. So are pictures.

Lady Butler lived from 1846 to 1933 and her story is so 'period' that I cannot resist giving it at some length.

Above·
Battle pictures have been popular from the earliest times and, *mutatis mutandis,* are still in great demand.
Narmer, King of Egypt, smiting his enemies, *c.* 3200 B.C.

Below:
Lord Lovat (Peter Lawford) leads his men across the Orne River. Shooting an heroic scene in Darryl F. Zanuck's film, *The Longest Day,* released by 20th Century-Fox.

She was born Elizabeth Thompson and had a delightful, free-and-easy childhood, spent partly in Italy and partly in England. Her mother was musical and artistic, and her father, a sensitive, cultured man of independent means, had decided, after failing to get into Parliament, to do nothing further except educate his two daughters. In this he was remarkably successful as one of them became the poetess Alice Meynell whose lyric 'She walks the lady of my delight, A shepherdess of sheep', used to occur in anthologies with such frequency that we cultivated a great loathing for her, while the other, Elizabeth, became a celebrated military artist.

What launched her on this particular line has not been recorded, but at the age of seven she was already drawing battles and once started, she went on. Affectionate parents gave her every encouragement and allowed her to attend various art schools where she worked with tremendous fervour. Her flair was for lightning sketches of men and horses, and with practice she was able to work these up into pictures which were accepted by exhibitions and found ready buyers.

The forceful personality of Miss Thompson (as it seems proper to call her) soon caused her to be surrounded by a circle of supporters and when in 1873 she was commissioned by a Mr. Galloway of Manchester to paint a large picture of a Crimean roll-call, her friends rallied round and helped her to find costumes and accoutrements in pawnshops and to hunt up ex-soldiers as models. She wanted to get every detail correct—what, for instance, were the badges on the pouches and the letters printed on the haversacks?—and the Crimean veterans were able to tell her everything, only unfortunately they often contradicted each other and also themselves. She painted on in a frenzy, and the picture was still wet when the time came for the At Home which was held in every self-respecting studio just before the Academy sending-in day.

A buttons was engaged to open the door, and for two days visitors streamed in, among them the agent for Mr. Galloway, who reported so favourably to Manchester that, though she had been promised only £100, she received a cheque for £126. It was the first proof that she had scored a bull's-eye.

Miss Thompson, who was by now twenty-seven, was wild with excitement and could not wait to hear how her picture was received at the Academy—her last year's offering had been skied, her others refused—so a friend asked one of the selection committee, a stranger to her, to write to her at once and tell her the worst. She received from this R.A. a most gratifying letter containing the remarkable sentence, 'I was so struck by the excellent work in it that I proposed we should lift our hats and give it, and you, a round of Huzzahs, which was generally done'.

Varnishing Day was a triumph. All the R.A. s crowded round to congratulate her. She wrote in her diary with charming frankness, 'I by no means disliked it all. Delightful is it to be an object of interest to so many people.'

Then came the Royalties' Private View and the Prince of Wales wanted to buy the picture but, of course, it was already bought and paid for by Mr. Galloway. The next day was the 'To-me-glorious Private View of 1874'.

I don't suppose I ever can have another such day (she wrote to her father) because however great my future successes may be, they can never partake of the character of this one. It is my first great success. . . . You know that 'the Elite of London society' goes to the Private View. Well, the greater part of the elite have been presented to me this day. . . . Galloway's tall figure was almost a fixture near the painting. That poor man, he was sadly distracted about the Prince of Wales affair, but the last I heard from him was that he *couldn't* part with it. Someone at the Academy offered him £1,000 for it, and T. Agnew told him he would give him anything he asked. . . . Do you remember joking with me, when I was a child, about the exaggerations of popularity? How strange it felt today to be realizing, in actual experience, what you warned me of, in fun. . . . You need not be afraid that I shall forget. What I do feel is great pleasure at having 'Arrived' at last. (Various people tried to pin her down to paint pictures for them and) Lady Somebody introduced me to Miss Florence Nightingale's sister, who wanted to know if there was any possibility of my 'most kindly' letting the picture be taken, at the close of the Exhibition, to her poor sister to see. Miss Nightingale, you know, is now bedridden. . . .

(*Diary*) *May 4th.*—The opening day at the Royal Academy. A dense crowd before my Grenadiers. . . . I may say that I awoke this morning and found myself famous. Great fun at the Academy, where some of my dear fellow students rejoicing in the fulfilment of their prophecies in the old days. Overwhelmed with congratulations on all sides; and as to papers, it is impossible to copy their magnificent critiques, from *The Times* downwards.

May 6th.—The Queen had my picture abstracted from the R.A. last night to gaze at, at Buckingham Palace! It is now, of course, in its place again.

Later on it was removed from the exhibition for a whole day and sent to Windsor so that the Queen could show it to the Tsar, and finally, after considerable haggling, the Queen got Mr. Galloway to give it up to her on the condition that she should sign six of the prints. Actually, he did quite well out of it financially as Miss Thompson promised him her next picture, copyright and all, for £1,126, and he was able to sell the copyright for £2,000. The *Roll-Call* copyright which she had kept herself she had been happy to sell for a mere £1,200.

The rest of the summer was to match. The Queen gave her a pearl and emerald bracelet. Generals assured her that the picture was right in every way. There was a policeman in front of it to move on the crowd and to protect inferior works from being crushed by people who were such gluttons for having their withers wrung that in another part of the gallery Luke Fildes's harrowing *Applicants for Admission to a Casual Ward* had to be protected by a rope. Her photograph sold a quarter of a million copies and she received a fan-mail including a poem beginning, 'Go on, go on, thou glorious girl'. Celebrities begged to be presented to her. Every night there was a dinner, a party or a ball. And the splendid thing was that she did not find that success was ashes between the teeth; she found it absolutely wonderful and said so.

'The grand and glorious Lord Mayor's banquet to the stars of literature and art came off today, July 21st, and it was to me such a delightful thing that I felt all the time in a pleasant sort of dream. . . . I wished the evening could have lasted a week. Although she sometimes had an uncomfortable feeling that her popularity was exaggerated she also felt that she had a power of touching 'the people's heart which does not change'.

The picture promised to Mr. Galloway was to be of Quatre Bras and Miss Thompson went to Aldershot, Chatham and Woolwich to watch manœuvres. Soldiers were marched in front of her, and they wheeled and fired as she requested, and she picked out the types she wanted as models. She had a Waterloo uniform made at the government clothing factory, using the baize cloth dyed the brick-dust red that was worn at that date. How exactly does one kneel to resist cavalry? And how to combine 'the drill book and the fierce fray'? At Henley she and her mother looked about for a suitable field of rye. Most of it had been cut but at last they found one, bought a patch and with the help of some children trampled it flat. The horses at Sangar's Circus lay down for her and at the Horseguards riding school a magnificent black charger had one of his legs strapped up and was then thrown down. 'How he plunged and snorted in clouds of dust till the final plunge, when the riding master and a trooper threw themselves on him to keep him down while I made a frantic sketch.' Later she got two troopers to charge straight at her.

All this is taken from Lady Butler's memoirs. She also describes how she came to paint *Scotland For Ever*. It was in 1879 and she had been to the Private View of that famous first exhibition at the Grosvenor Gallery, where could be seen the works of artists like Burne Jones, Watts, Holman Hunt, and Tissot.

The Grosvenor was the home of the Aesthetes of the period whose sometimes unwholesome productions preceded those of our modern 'Impressionists'. I felt myself getting more and more annoyed while perambulating these rooms, and to such a point of exasperation was I compelled that I fairly fled and, breathing the honest air of Bond Street, took a hansom to my studio. There I pinned a seven foot sheet of brown paper on an old canvas and, with a piece of charcoal and a piece of white chalk, flung the charge of 'The Greys' upon it.

In 1877 she married an eminent Irish soldier, Sir William Butler. The marriage was a great success. She was already a keen Roman Catholic and she took kindly to Ireland. Her husband was indulgent and though they moved from place to place and often held official positions and though they had six children, her painting career does not seem to have been impeded for a moment. Taking an eight foot canvas to Egypt and back was nothing to her.

Lady Butler (Elizabeth Thompson), (1846–1933)

Scotland for Ever!, 1881. Lady Butler (Leeds Art Gallery)
The charge of the Scots Greys at Waterloo. 'I twice saw a charge of the Greys before painting *Scotland for Ever!* . . . I stood in front to see them coming on. One cannot, of course, stop too long to see them close . . .'

Calling the Roll after an Engagement, Crimea (generally known as *The Roll Call*), 1874. Lady Butler
(Reproduced by gracious permission of Her Majesty the Queen)
Painted nineteen years after the end of the Crimean War when the artist was twenty-seven, it was cheered by the Hanging Committee of the Royal Academy and bought by Queen Victoria. It is now in the Officer's Mess at Camberley.

The Remnants of an Army, 1879. Lady Butler (Tate Gallery)
The end of the British retreat from Cabul in 1842. 'One man alone reached Jellalabad to tell the tale. Literally one man, Dr. Brydon, came to Jellalabad out of a moving host which had numbered in all some sixteen thousand when it set out on its march.' (Justin McCarthy, *History of Our Own Times*.)

The Race of Riderless Horses down the main street of Rome. Sketch by Lady Butler, 1870

Bishops going to the Vatican. Sketch by **Lady** Butler, 1870

Faithful Unto Death, 1865. Sir Edward Poynter, Bt., P.R.A. (1836–1919) (Walker Art Gallery, Liverpool) 'In carrying out the excavations near the Herculaneum Gate of Pompeii, the skeleton of a soldier in full armour was discovered. Forgotten in the terror and confusion that reigned during the destruction of the city, the sentinel had received no order to quit his post, and while all sought their safety in flight, he remained faithful to his duty, notwithstanding the certain doom which awaited him.'

When the 1914 war broke out Lady Butler was in the middle of yet another picture of Waterloo, but rising to the occasion she at once began making sketches of modern soldiers. Her sons went to the Front and for the first time she seems to have noticed that war had its unpleasant side. However, she was still a military artist and she rushed round observing troops minutely, determined as ever to get it all absolutely correct, and her industry and energy were rewarded by the success of her two shows of water-colours.

Lady Butler's last years were spent in Ireland at the house of a married daughter, and it all sounds like a thoroughly satisfactory and enjoyable and well-run life. Perhaps she should have died earlier, before her style of painting had gone out of fashion, but how lucky she was to be born when she was! Nowadays, troops may be marched, guns fired, horses thrown down, for a film unit; definitely not for a young lady with a sketch book.

★   ★   ★

Besides soldiers there were knights, the aftermath of the Victorian passion for King Arthur, and of *The Idylls of the King*, and *Parsifal* and the Pre-Raphaelites. The most conspicuous object in Eton College Chapel was *Sir Galahad* by Watts, and in the dining-room of the indifferent school where I spent one term there hung Poynter's picture of the Roman sentry who stood at his post while Vesuvius was erupting. I do not know whether the boys liked Sir Galahad. The Roman sentry had dated and was simply not noticed;

I expect he was soon succeeded by sunflowers, and after that by ducks and ballet girls and wild horses.

The point about knights was that they represented the strong who were supposed to protect the weak, and in an inarticulate way this equally held good of all soldiers. I know a cottage where a large coloured portrait of Lord Roberts still presides as a sort of patron saint—St. George perhaps. Weapons and uniform, one's sword and 'the guns' one knew to be symbols of a sacred trust, though it would have been very embarrassing to put it into words, and when books did so we were revolted. As far as I remember, *Daddy's Sword* was quite readable but the subject we felt was in excruciating taste. Some of our most firmly held beliefs we never expressed because the necessary words were so frightful and even facetious circumlocutions had become impossible and were only found in fiction. We went hot all over when it was reported that the mother of one of our friends had told the governess that criticizing her behind her back was 'not cricket'. But our *patois* was fraught with pitfalls—it was appalling to use 'honourable' but 'dishonourable' was all right.

Questions of honour and courage exercised our minds a good deal. Goody-goody books were out and religion was taboo, and those writers who wished to improve the young harped on heroism. One was always having Arctic explorers rammed down one's throat, especially that very gallant gentleman Captain Oates, and one wondered if one would be brave if the house caught fire or one was tortured for the faith. At any rate I was all set to sing *Nearer My God to Thee* if there was a wreck.

We distinguished between giving your word and giving your promise, and my sister invented grades of lies to be used in emergency—there was an ordinary white lie, of course, and a copper lie to save your own life and a silver lie to save the life of a friend and a gold lie to save the life of an enemy.

I suppose these preoccupations were in the air and were nursery versions of what was being discussed in the drawing-room. Low-brows read *The Four Feathers* and high-brows *Lord Jim*. The grown-ups must have felt tremendously secure, they were so sure of the way to deal with circumstances in which they did not expect to find themselves. Little as I heard about the outside world, the story of the couple who had behaved so badly on the *Titanic* worked through to me, and when the war came one looked askance not only at the men who 'didn't do too well' but also at their relatives. My mother had an inexhaustible supply of anecdotes about people who 'nobody spoke to' because of something they had done in love, war or the City. (It was noticeable that in the Second World War when civilians felt that it might be their turn next, they were less ready to make accusations of cowardice. Also that the cynics of the twenties and thirties rose to the occasion and were stupendously brave.)

Another bequest of the knights, or, if not of the knights, of the Pre-Raphaelites, was a vague idea that the highest form of love was a remote Dante-Beatrice relationship. It was very nebulous and I was too young to understand it, but I fancy that in the early years of the century it was easier than it is now to get the wavelength of that curious work, the *Vita Nuova*, and that some of the extraordinary letters written by Edwardian socialites were deliberate attempts to live beautifully on a Dante-esque plane. Myself, I knew I would

Sir Galahad. G. F. Watts, O.M., R.A. (1817–1904). (Formerly in Eton College Chapel, now in the Watts Gallery, Compton, near Guildford)

The original was painted in 1862 and is in the Fogg Museum, Harvard. Some thirty years later Watts made this replica for Mr. Luxmoore of Eton and it occupied a conspicuous position in the College Chapel until recently when it was felt to be old-fashioned and was rusticated to the Watts Gallery.

The model for the figure was a schoolboy, Arthur Prinsep, whose parents were friends and patrons of Watts and who afterwards joined the Bengal Lancers and rose to be a Major-General. The Eton boys, of course, preferred to believe that it had been drawn from Ellen Terry. Perhaps this legend was based on the fact that, during her brief marriage to Watts, Ellen Terry did pose for a picture called *The Watcher* wearing a suit of armour. According to her own account she was so happy to be of service that she never noticed that it was heavy until she fainted.

never be up to it, and looking round the county it did not seem that anyone was getting very near. Much more dispiriting was the discovery that not only could one see no Parsifals on the horizon, but there also seemed to be a complete absence of Romeos. Married couples got along quite well together, but where was romance?

*   *   *

Just before my seventh birthday it was revealed that we had been making a mistake and that what we had believed to be modern times was merely a preamble. Modern times began in earnest with the war, THE war, the war which is the watershed between then and now.

For once, distance has not lent enchantment to the view. Nobody, nowadays, has a good word to say for it, while when it was actually in progress highly intelligent people thought it was serving a useful purpose. Sherlock Holmes, by that time an elderly man, was undismayed.

'There's an East wind coming . . .' (he said at the beginning of August 1914) 'such a wind as never blew on England yet. It will be cold and bitter, Watson, and a good many of us may wither before its blast. But it's God own wind none the less, and a cleaner, better, stronger land will be in the sunshine when the storm has cleared.'

Rupert Brooke, the white hope of English poetry, also welcomed war as a release and a purification. 'Now God be thanked who has matched us with this hour . . .' he wrote, and in another sonnet, 'Honour has come back, as a king to earth . . .'. Julian Grenfell, an aristocrat, born into the *milieu* of the Souls, welcomed it too in a poem, *Into Battle*, which was much read and loved. Even the Cambridge professor A. E. Housman, who normally took rather a sarcastic view of the efforts of the British Army, in a few winged words spoke up for the dead who had 'saved the sum of things'. I admit the horrors of trench life were pointed out by poets like Siegfried Sassoon, and as the months rolled on the exalted mood wore off, but I think I am right in saying that to the end people remained, incredible as it may seem, extraordinarily *jolly*.

After it was all over my governess gave me to understand that, before the war, society had been very decadent and that the war had been more or less what had been needed. I do not know of whom she was thinking when she said 'society' but perhaps she had been reading one of my mother's favourite authors, Saki, whose world was certainly ripe for annihilation. Her remark should not, however, be dismissed as utterly silly, and one should remember, too, the spinsters of England, who were able to make their great gaol-break not only without giving offence but positively with honour.

Myself, I have always voted with the optimists—damn it all, isn't Hope a virtue, classed with Faith and Charity?—and I cannot forgive Sir Edward Grey for his famous dirge, 'The lamps are going out all over Europe: we shall not see them lit again in our lifetime'.

Did he consider, just because he could go abroad without a passport, that he was living in a demi-paradise and that his Edwardian Age was so perfect that any change must be for the worse? Everything I read about that time makes me think that the world is better now. And if I get depressed by the newspapers with their marvellous machinery for collecting bad news from every corner of the globe and serving it up hot for breakfast, I can always

109

cheer myself up by thinking of the villages of today with their well-fed, well-dressed children pushed in modish prams by smart young mothers with the latest hair style, and compare them to the pinched and pasty-faced little gnomes dragged along by drudges in sacking aprons and men's cloth caps whom I used to see when I was a child myself, half a century ago. In this respect, at least, the lamps are incomparably brighter than they used to be.

FINALE

Other Days, Other Poets

I WILL conclude this excursion into the past with a poem which was a favourite with my mother and her friends. It begins, 'A child in the nursery crying . . .' and they quoted it to each other and copied it into albums. One of my uncles had found it in a magazine and the author was supposed to have been the sporting novelist Whyte-Melville, who is so forgotten nowadays that perhaps I should add a few words to explain who he was and what he represented.

My mother grew up in the days when horses were, of necessity, part of the background of life and hunting and racing were the natural occupations of a leisured gentleman; and although she herself preferred to follow the hounds on foot, the complete works of Whyte-Melville had an honoured place among her neat rows of collected editions. Sometimes as a treat she would lend us one of his novels but we did not respond with much enthusiasm and I was never sufficiently interested to ask her about the author.

Consulting the invaluable *Dictionary of National Biography* I find that his life was in many ways different from that of the average novelist. G. J. Whyte-Melville was born in 1821. Father a wealthy Scotch landowner. Mother a duke's daughter. Eton. Coldstream Guards. During Crimean War a Major in Turkish Irregular Cavalry. Unhappily married to daughter of a peer. Strain of melancholy runs through his books. Hunting his main interest and occupation. Avoided literary circles. Refused to take his writing seriously and gave his profits to charities such as reading-rooms for grooms in hunting quarters. 'An acknowledged arbiter of hunting practice and a critic of costume, he was careless to a fault in his own attire.' In 1878 killed out hunting.

As it happens, we have a set of Whyte-Melville in the attic of the house where I now live. They were bought at a sale by my husband under the erroneous impression that as he liked hunting he would enjoy reading them. One of the volumes is called *Songs and Verses* but it does not include 'A child in the nursery crying'. However, it is illustrated, and I am amused to find that the pictures (dated '98) are signed by none other than S. E. Waller (who painted, you remember, *The Day of Reckoning*).

So we are back where we started, at the turn of the century, when my mother was an enthusiastic girl in a white satin ball-gown (to be strictly accurate the article of attire which she treasured as a romantic souvenir was a boater with a brigade ribbon), and Malmaison carnations were so large that they had to have their heads supported by a circle of pink cardboard. Of course, one can see now that *The Day of Reckoning* and Whyte-Melville's

1899

The Wish Tower. 1903. James Sant, R.A. (1820–1916)

Digby Grand go together perfectly; they are both a sort of mild Thackeray-and-horses, slightly sententious, slightly humorous, slightly sentimental, with here and there a bit that is extremely lifelike.

But I still have not found 'A child in the nursery crying', so I appeal as before to my mother's old friend Mrs. B. and she says, Yes, of course she has got it. My mother wrote it out for her and she pasted it into Whyte-Melville's *Songs* which we find on a top shelf among her other choicely bound books of poetry and I sit down to make a copy.

Written, I suppose, in the eighteen seventies, and current for the next thirty years, it turns out to be a low murmur of despair. Do not imagine however, that I am suggesting that my mother and her friends were morbid. I am sure that they were no more depressed by it than you, dear reader, are disturbed by all the poems and pictures which today are described as 'disturbing'. It is only natural for cheerful youth to enjoy declaiming 'It is a tale told by an idiot', or to quote brightly Albert Chevalier's 'Wot's the Good of Hanyfink? Why, Nuffink'. Nor do I pretend that it is great poetry. I offer it merely as an unambitious little jingle which took the fancy of a group of young Victorio-Edwardians as they looked round eagerly at the world, and tried to make sense of what they saw.

LINES WRITTEN IN DEJECTION

Ascribed to G. J. Whyte-Melville

A child in the nursery crying,
A boy in the cricket field—out,
A youth for a fantasy sighing,
A man with a fit of the gout.
A heart dried up and narrowed,
A task repeated in vain,
A field ploughed up and harrowed
And bare and barren of grain.
Some sense of experience wasted,
Of counsel misunderstood,
Of pleasure, bitter when tasted,
And of pain that did him no good.
Some sparks of sentiment perished,
Some flashes of genius lost,
A torrent of false love cherished,
A ripple of true love crossed.
Some feeble breasting of trouble
To glide again with the stream,
Of principle void as a bubble,
In practice vague as a dream.
A future hope half-hearted,

113

For dim is the future now
That the triple cord has parted
And death is damp on the brow.
And a debt to pay to the debtor—
A doctor, a surgeon, a nurse—
A feeling he should have been better,
A doubt if he could have been worse.
While the ghostly finger traces
The ghostly figure of Doom
And troops of ghostly faces
Pace on in the darkened room,
With ghostly shapes to beckon,
And ghostly voices to call,
And a grim Recorder to reckon
And add up the total of all.
The sum of a life expended,
A pearl in a pig-trough cast,
A comedy, played and ended,
And what has it come to at last?
The dead man propped on a pillow,
The journey taken alone,
The tomb with an urn and a willow,
And a lie carved deep on the stone.

"I'D A LEAD OF THEM ALL WHEN WE CAME TO THE BROOK."

THE END